ENGLISH
MATTERS 2

CLARE CONSTANT · SUSAN DUBERLEY

Heinemann

Contents

Spelling resource sheets will be found on pages 51–79 of the Teacher's File.

Throughout this book you will find the following cross-references:

TRF The Teacher's File provides support for the activity.
PAGES 00–00

SKILLS The Skills Book offers skills practice related to the activity.
PAGES 00–00

SEE ALSO Other pages in the book will help you with the activity.
PAGES 00–00

The activities in this book have been colour coded:

- specific speaking and listening: pink

- reading: yellow

- writing: blue

- specific language work: green.

This is me!

1.1
TRF
PAGE 12

Read this star profile. Then answer the questions below.

'JAM' ON THE SOFA

What do you do to relax?
I curl up in front of a video with a plate of crispy bacon and peanut butter sandwiches – or I go clubbing with my mates. We usually go to Rocky's.

Which is your favourite film, and why?
It's got to be *Cliffhanger*. All those shots of mountains and people falling off them are really scary.

What makes you cry?
Seeing news stories about starving children in the Sudan on TV. It really gets to me, especially when I think how rich we are in this country.

Jamie Dolan

1 List three things Jamie enjoys.

2 Why is Jamie upset by some news stories?

3 Describe the way the article has been set out on the page.
The heading is at … so that you know …
The photograph is beside … It shows you who …
The caption is under … It tells you …
The questions are … The answers are …

1.2

Write five questions to ask someone in a star profile. Use one item from each box in each question. For example:

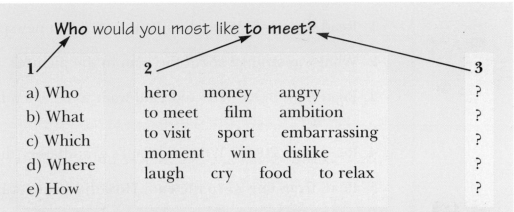

Who would you most like **to meet?**

1	2	3
a) Who	hero money angry	?
b) What	to meet film ambition	?
c) Which	to visit sport embarrassing	?
d) Where	moment win dislike	?
e) How	laugh cry food to relax	?

Check that all your questions start with a capital letter and end with a question mark.

1.3

TRF
PAGE 12

SKILLS
PAGES 4–5

Work in pairs. You are going to do a 'star profile' for a teenage magazine. Take it in turns with a partner to ask your questions. Write down the most important words in their answers.

What is your favourite sport?

I really like **football**. I **support** Arsenal. They're bound **to win the FA cup** this year because …

1.4

TRF
PAGE 12

Use your notes to write the star profile. Set it out like the one opposite. Write in sentences.

1.5

Read the passage on the opposite page, about Paul Zindel. Then answer the questions below. Write in sentences.

1 Read lines 1–8. What does Paul look for in newspapers?

2 What was strange about the man in the picture?

3 Read lines 9–15. Who did Paul want to be when he was younger?

4 Read lines 20–26. What did Paul's grandfather die from?

5 Read from line 27 to the end. How did Paul get his little scar?

1.6

Work in pairs. Discuss each sentence below. Is it true or false? Which lines in the text show this?

1 Paul's family were well off.

2 Paul liked playing jokes on people.

3 Paul wanted exciting things to happen to him.

4 Some of Paul's family have lived in America.

1.7

SKILLS

PAGES 6–7

The things on and next to Paul's desk tell you seven more biographical points about him. Write down what they are.

1 Paul has a dog called ...   2 He likes to grow ...

The Pigman and Me

I've always liked strange things.
For example, I am the only kid
I know who likes looking through
newspapers for weird news. When
5 I find a shocking story or picture
I save it. This week I have cut out
a picture of a man who was born
with feet like a monkey.

There are eight **biographical points**
10 about me you should know straight away:

1) My sister taught me how to cut out fake coins
   from cardboard. She also showed me how to shape
   lamb chops out of clay. We never had much real
   money or food.

15 2) I once wanted to be Batman and fly off buildings.

3) I longed to be kidnapped by aliens and taken for
   a ride in their flying saucer.

4) I once prayed to own a pet gorilla.

5) I used to enjoy playing tricks on people, like
20 putting drawing pins on their seats.

6) When my father's father was sixteen, he got a job
   on a Dutch ship. When they reached America, he
   jumped off the boat and swam to Staten Island. He
   got married and opened a baker's shop. He and
25 his wife died from eating too many crumbcakes
   before I could meet them.

7) A truck once ran over my left elbow. It really hurt
   and left a little scar.

8) I am afraid I will one day die by shark attack.

Adapted from *The Pigman and Me* by Paul Zindel

biographical points – things about me and my life

1.8

Work in pairs. Read the advertisement opposite. Then search through it for the following information.

1 List all the people in Sakhina's family.

2 Find two sentences which show that the family is poor.

3 List six different jobs Sakhina does for her family.

4 List three ways World Vision tries to help families like Sakhina's.

5 What can you and your friends do to help people like Sakhina?

1.9

TRF
PAGE 13

SKILLS
PAGES 8–9

Use the information you have gathered. Write a leaflet to make people want to go without food for 24 hours to raise money for World Vision. Follow these steps.

Panel 1

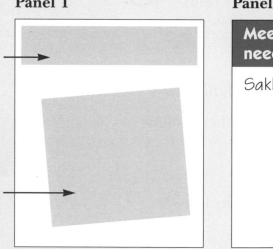

Make up a heading which 'grabs' the reader's attention. Put it here.

Put an eye-catching picture here.

Panel 2

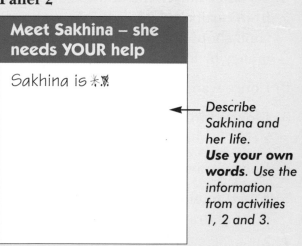

Meet Sakhina – she needs YOUR help

Sakhina is

 *Describe Sakhina and her life. **Use your own words**. Use the information from activities 1, 2 and 3.*

Panel 3

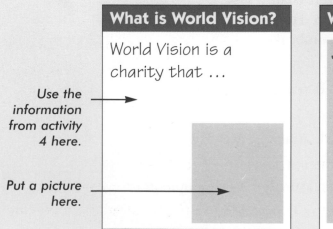

What is World Vision?

World Vision is a charity that …

Use the information from activity 4 here.

Put a picture here.

Panel 4

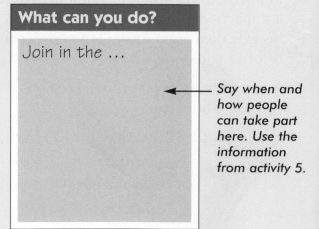

What can you do?

Join in the …

Say when and how people can take part here. Use the information from activity 5.

Every 24 hours for Sakhina is a struggle

Sakhina is seven. She lives in the biggest slum in Bangladesh. Every day she has to care for her sick father. She also looks after her younger brother and sister.

Six o'clock: Sakhina gets up. Her first job is to sweep the house. She then washes herself and the dishes in the pond nearby. The water is filthy and has **sewage** in it.

Eleven o'clock: Sakhina walks five kilometres to the clothing factory where her two older sisters work. She takes their lunch which she made earlier.

Two o'clock: Sakhina arrives home to wash the clothes and sweep the house again. Then it's off to market to buy whatever food the family can afford.

Six o'clock: Sakhina cleans the stove and prepares food for the whole family.

Nine o'clock: Sakhina's mother and sisters return from work. The family eats together and Sakhina goes to bed.

Could you go without food for 24 hours on 20th March?

Get your friends and family to sponsor you. Then you can help World Vision give people like Sakhina **vaccinations** and **healthcare**.

We also help families earn enough money to feed their children.

24 hours in your life is all it takes to help someone like Sakhina.

Send for your FREE 24 Hour Famine kit today.

24 HOUR FAMINE

sewage – waste which would usually go down a toilet

vaccinations – injections that stop people getting diseases

healthcare – visits to doctors and dentists, and taking medicine

1.10 Read the poem on the opposite page. Then answer the questions below.

1.11

TRF
PAGES 14, 78

SKILLS
PAGE 11

Work in pairs. What do the words below from the poem mean? Use a dictionary to find out. Write each word in a sentence.

1 fractious

2 insufferable

3 juvenile

4 opinionated

1.12 Work in a small group. Discuss lines 26–30.

1 What is wrong with the letters beginning lines 26–27?

2 Who do you think is saying lines 28–30?

3 Is this a good way to end this poem? Why?

1.13

TRF
PAGES 14, 79

SKILLS
PAGE 12

Work in pairs. Use a thesaurus. Find three words which mean the same as the words below. Write them down.

1 cheerful   2 generous   3 charming

1.14

TRF
PAGE 14

Write your own A–Z poem saying how wonderful teenagers are. You may like to use some words from the box. Start it like this:

They're   **a**greeable and
            behave well
            cheerful and always …

independent
joking   quite …
valuable   (e)xciting
zany

A Parents' and Teenagers' Alphabet Book

*They're   **a**ggravating
                belly-aching
                crying out loud and always
                driving up the wall.

5   *They're   **e**dgy
                fractious
                grouchy and always getting on a
                high horse.

*They're   **i**nsufferable
10   **j**uvenile, don't
                keep their hair on and always
                laying down the law.

*They're   **m**addening
                never satisfied
15   **o**pinionated and always
                pointing the finger.

*They're   **q**uick-tempered
                ratty
                sulky and always ready to
20   **t**ake offence

*They're   **u**nco-operative
                very scratchy
                wearing and always e
                xtremely moody.

25   And
*They're   **u**nsociable and
                boring.

But those last two lines don't begin with
Y and Z that's just what I'd expect
30 *from you you can't even be bothered to …*

Adapted from a poem by David Crystal

* Choose who you think the description
is about – parents or teenagers?

Kinds of sentence

There are four kinds of sentence.

Will the bodybuilder keep his balance?	That's amazing!	He's broken the world record.	Please move over there. Get out of the way!
Question	**Exclamation**	**Statement**	**Directive**

1 **Questions** ask about something. They end with a question mark: ?

2 **Exclamations** show surprise, shock or anger. They end with an exclamation mark: !

3 **Statements** tell someone something. They end with a full stop: .

4 **Directives** tell someone to do something. They end with an exclamation mark: ! or full stop: .

1.15 Read about this world record.

It really happened! A man called John Evans balanced 100 bricks on his head for 14 seconds. When was this? It was on the 18th November 1996 at London Zoo in England. Don't try this yourself!

1.16 Check through the passage above and copy out:

1 a question sentence

2 an exclamation sentence

3 a statement sentence

4 a directive sentence

1.17

Look at the cartoon below. David Huxley is breaking a world record. Write a different *kind* of sentence for each speech bubble.

1 Write a directive sentence for picture 1.

2 Write a question sentence for picture 2.

3 Write a statement sentence for picture 3.

4 Write an exclamation sentence for picture 4.

TRF
PAGE 15

SKILLS
PAGE 13

Check that all your sentences:

- make sense
- begin with a capital letter

- end with one of these:
  full stop   .
  question mark   ?
  exclamation mark !

The way I see it

2.1 Read the passage opposite, then answer the questions below. Estelle is all dressed up and ready to go to Fiends disco. Her parents are horrified.

2.2 Work in pairs. Estelle and her parents have different points of view. What are they? Record your ideas in a chart like the one below.

Views about:	Estelle's opinion	Parents' opinion
Estelle's clothes	She has taken a lot of trouble with her appearance (shown by lines 1–9).	They hate them. Mum calls them 'horrible' in line 12.
What Estelle is old enough to do at her age		

2.3 Estelle's mum writes to a problem page in a magazine for advice. She explains their different opinions. Use your chart to help you write her letter.

TRF
PAGE 18

SKILLS
PAGES 14–15

SEE ALSO
PAGE 20

Dear Cathy
I'm so worried about my daughter Estelle. She's only 14 but **she thinks** it's OK to wear ...
I think ...
She also thinks she should be allowed to ... because ...
I think ... because ...

All Dressed Up and Ready to Go …

Estelle looked as if she'd stepped out of a horror film. She might have been **Dracula's** daughter. She was dressed all in black: black blouse, black skirt, black **fishnet tights**. When I say 'dressed', I'm being generous, because the blouse was
5 slipping off her shoulders, the skirt was all fringe, and the holes in her tights were enormous. Around her neck hung yards of silver chain. As for the silver belt, it was made from lots of jagged splinters. When Estelle moved it caught the light. It was quite painful to look at.
10 Mum went mad.

'Listen to me, young lady. You can go straight upstairs and take off those horrible clothes. If you think for one moment that your father and I are going to let you walk out of this house looking like *that* – '
15 Words failed Mum for a moment. Estelle took her chance.

'Look, Mum!' she said, 'I'm not a baby. I'm me. And I'm old enough to go out with my friends.'

'You're not old enough to go to Fiends Discotheque.'
20 'Why not?'

'Because we've heard all about it, that's why!' Dad broke in sharply. 'And we've seen the types hanging around outside, smoking, and swigging from their beer cans. And *worse*.'
25 Estelle stuck her hands on her hips.

'I'm not too young. I'm not! You just don't understand how things are these days. *Everyone* in my year is allowed to smoke. *Everyone's* allowed to drink. And *everyone's* allowed to go to
30 the discotheque. I've made arrangements. You can't treat me like a baby. You have to let me go! You can't keep me locked up.'

Adapted from *The Book of the Banshee*
by Anne Fine

Dracula – a vampire who dressed in black
Fishnet tights – black tights made with big holes

2.4 Read the TV script opposite. Tyke wants to help her friend Danny to do well in an important test. She has stolen a copy of the test paper.

2.5 Answer the questions below.

> 1 Read lines 1–8. What is Tyke asking Beryl to do?
>
> 2 Read lines 9–16. Why does Tyke want to help Danny?
>
> 3 Do you think that Tyke is doing the right thing?

2.6

SKILLS
PAGE 17

Now read the stage directions again. They are in blue italics.

> 1 Stage directions tell the actors what to do. They also show what the audience will hear and see. Which directions:
> - show what the audience will **hear**?
> - show what the audience will **see**?
>
> 2 How do you know this play was not written for radio?

2.7

TRF
PAGE 17

Scene 2 has been started for you, opposite. Write the rest of the scene. Set it out like this.

Character's name   *Speech begins with a capital letter*

Colon

> TYKE: Let's go through these questions together, Danny. You sit over there on the bed.

You could continue with:
- Tyke's dad coming in
- Beryl coming to the rescue.

2.8 Now write a television stage direction for the *start* of scene 2.

> 1 Say **which characters** are in the start of the scene.
>
> 2 Say **where** the characters are.
>
> 3 Say what the audience will **hear**.
>
> 4 Say what the audience will **see**.

The Turbulent Term of Tyke Tyler

Scene 1

Beryl's bedroom in Tyke's home. Pop music is playing loudly. BERYL is putting on make up in front of her mirror. There is a knock at the door. TYKE enters.

5   TYKE: Please help me with this test. Check the answers for me.

BERYL turns, reads the test paper, is shocked, turns down volume of music.

BERYL: Tyke, that's cheating. Take it back quick before you get into trouble.

TYKE: I'm not cheating. I'm doing this for Danny, not me. If he
10   can't get good marks he'll have to go to another school.

BERYL: Are you sure he'll have to change school?

TYKE: 'Cross my heart and hope to die,
          Drop down dead if I tell a lie.'

BERYL sighs.

15 BERYL: OK. But we mustn't let anyone know, or all hell will break out.

TYKE *(simply)*: Thanks, Berry.

BERYL *(reading)*: Write two words from the passage which mean the same as 'large' …

20 *BERYL helps Tyke with the questions.*

> Adapted from the TV script of *The Turbulent Term of Tyke Tyler*
> by Gene Kemp, adapted by Richard Callanan

A possible start for Scene 2

TYKE: Let's go through these questions together, Danny. You sit over there on the bed.

DANNY: Thanks, Tyke.

TYKE: The two words which mean the same as 'large' are 'enormous' and 'massive' …

TYKE stops as she hears her dad's footsteps outside the door.

DAD: What's …

2.9

Read the poem on the opposite page. Then answer the questions below.

1 What does the postman think he delivers?

2 Who gets sadness?

3 Why is Benny bored?

4 Why does Mr Wilde's post make him angry?

5 What is surprising about Ethne's post?

2.10

Work in pairs. Stanzas (verses) 3–7 follow a pattern. Change the sentences below so they say what that pattern is.

1 The last line tells you who receives the letter.
  The first line tells you who receives the letter.

2 The last word of each stanza is a feeling.

3 Only the second line of a stanza says what was in the letter.

2.11

Work in a group. Write a poem with the same pattern.

Instead of a postman it should be the person who runs the letters page in your favourite magazine. You could choose feelings from the box below.

You could start your poem like this:

I don't receive letters
Says the letters page editor,
I receive emotions.

Take this morning.

Frustration from Ed –
Why was the football on
At the same time as EastEnders?

delight	anger	jealousy	disappointment
worry	hope	surprise	

The Postman

1 'I don't deliver letters,'
Says our postman,
'I deliver emotions.

2 Take this morning.

3 Happiness for Jason –
He's been asked for a trial
For the local schools' football team.

4 Sadness for Glory Roberts –
A cousin has died peacefully
In his sleep.

5 Boredom for Benny –
Another special offer
Cut-price double glazing.

6 Anger for Mr Wilde –
A gas bill
He just can't believe.

7 Love for Ethne –
A Valentine
On an autumn day.

8 They look like letters,'
Says our postman,
'But it's a sackful of emotions.'

By Jennifer and Graeme Curry

Facts and opinions

1 An **opinion** is somebody's point of view:

   He is really mean!

2 A **fact** is a piece of information that you can check is true:

   Tom has won five million pounds.

2.12

Read the article below.

TOM HIGGINS, aged 34, of 5, Oak Terrace, Toddington, won the lottery last Saturday. His prize was over five million pounds.

5   Tom said, 'I just picked any old numbers. I think believing some numbers are lucky is a load of rubbish.' He hasn't decided what to do with his winnings yet. 'I'm just going
10 to wait and see,' he said, 'but whatever happens I'll still carry on being a teacher. It's a wonderful job.'

But Tom's wife Jo is sure they'll have a lot of fun. 'He's such a
15 generous bloke,' she said. 'He rushed down the pub on Saturday and bought everyone drinks. Then he took me out for a lovely meal.'

And Tom has promised Jo they will
20 be going on a luxury cruise for this year's holiday. 'It'll be great to get away together and decide what to do with all this money!' Tom said.

2.13

Make a note of the following facts from the article.

1 Read lines 1–4. How old is Tom and where does he live?

2 How much did he win?

3 Read lines 13–23. What did he do on Saturday?

4 What has he promised Jo?

2.14

Now find these opinions.

1 Read lines 5–12. What is Tom's opinion about lucky numbers?

2 What is Tom's opinion of his job?

3 Read lines 13–18. What is Jo's opinion of Tom?

2.15

Write down five facts about the National Lottery. Use complete sentences. Start each sentence in a different way.

1 The Lottery numbers are drawn twice a week.
2 You can buy tickets from …

2.16

Your friend has won £50,000 on the Lottery. She is thinking about how to spend the money. Write down your opinion of each of her ideas.

1 I think she should go on a cruise. It's a once in a lifetime …

2 I think she should save it, rather than fritter it away …

Nouns and noun phrases

2.17

Read the passage below. Find and copy out the phrases (groups of words) which describe:

1 what the lead singer looks like: The long-haired boy

2 the weather: the ...

3 the audience: the ...

The long-haired boy was about to sing his leading song. He stood on the stage in the blazing sunshine. Then he played a few notes on his gold electric guitar. At once the screaming teenage fans became quiet. Seeing their favourite group 'Wild Animal' play in the grounds of London Zoo was an experience they would never forget!

T R F

PAGE 19

The phrases you have written out are called **noun phrases**.

1 A **noun** is the name of something. It is a single word:

the **boy** played his **guitar**
　　↑　　　　　　↑
　　noun　　　　*noun*

2 A **noun phrase** is the group of words which includes the noun. It tells you more than a noun on its own.

The long-haired boy played **his gold electric guitar**.
　↗　　　　　　　　　　　　　↗
noun phrase　　　　　　*noun phrase*

Noun phrases make your work more interesting to read. They give you more detail about the noun.

2.18 Read the passage below. The nouns are in bold. Re-write the passage and turn them into noun phrases. Use the words in the box below to help you.

I saw **an evil looking man** ...

I saw _____ **man** jump up on _____ **stage** and grab _____ **guitar**. Then one of _____ **bouncers** came and pulled him away. _____ **audience** were screaming, 'Get him off! Get him off!'

| the front of the | The excited | an evil looking |
| Jack's expensive new | the tall strong | |

2.19

PAGE 20

Look at the cartoon. Write five sentences about what is happening. Use noun phrases in each sentence and underline them.

1 <u>The red-haired drummer</u> is looking in horror at <u>the long slithering stripy snake.</u>

THE WAY I SEE IT ◆ UNIT 2 23

UNIT 3 Looking good?

3.1

Read the passage opposite, then answer the questions below. Johnny needed a pair of green swimming trunks to enter the school diving competition and impress his friend Bosie. His Gran knitted him a pair.

1 Read lines 1–11. What happens to woollen trunks in water?

2 Read lines 12–24. How does Johnny feel when he first climbs on the platform?

3 How does Johnny feel just before he dives?

4 Read lines 25–30. Why does the elastic on Johnny's trunks snap?

3.2

The highlighted words show where the writer exaggerated. He made things sound worse than they were to make the story more amusing. In pairs, copy and complete the chart below for each phrase.

Description	What is exaggerated	Why it is funny
Lines 4–5	How much water the trunks soak up	It makes you picture the trunks as huge sponges.

3.3

SKILLS
PAGE 23

Think of something funny or embarrassing that happened to you or someone you know, or make something up. Write it as a story.

1 First plan your story. Put the events in the right order.

2 Decide which *details* you will exaggerate to make the story more amusing. *How* will you exaggerate them?

3 Now write your story.

Johnny Casanova

'Divers in the pool, please,' said the man on the **tannoy**.
I struggled to my feet and jumped in. I didn't imagine
what was going to happen next. You know how a single
sponge can soak up a bucket of water? Well, woollen
5 trunks are over fifty times worse. Over the next few
seconds they not only sucked up the water faster than a
troop of thirsty elephants, but they grew as well.
I had to be helped out of the pool. The trunks were
so long that they dragged along the tiles. They were
10 so heavy that my knees buckled twice on the way round
to the diving tower.

It took me fifteen minutes to climb forty-three steps.
By the time I reached the platform I was sweating and
totally **exhausted**. I staggered towards the edge of the
15 diving board and looked down. It was terrifying, like
standing on the top of **Niagara Falls**. I felt giddy and
would have tumbled forward but I was firmly rooted to
the platform by half a mile of sodden green knitwear.

I closed my eyes and raised my arms above my head.
20 This was it! I had to put the embarrassment of my
swimming trunks behind me. I needed to impress Bosie
and win her heart. I took a deep breath. Then I flew up
into the air, one forward roll, then a second, a twist, a
turn and then another.

25 My trunks were just too heavy. With a twang that
ricocheted off the glass roof, the knicker elastic snapped.
The trunks shot upwards off my waist like a **released
parachute** and followed me down into the water.

My entry into the pool was perfect, but I had no
30 clothes on.

Adapted from *The Changing Face of Johnny Casanova* by Jamie Rix

tannoy – loudspeakers
exhausted – very tired
Niagara Falls – very high waterfall in America
ricocheted – bounced
released parachute – a parachute that has opened

3.4 Read the passage opposite. People in China in the nineteenth century thought small feet were beautiful. Jung Chang's grandmother had her feet bound to stop them becoming too big.

3.5 Write two paragraphs in your own words. In the first describe how feet were bound. In the second explain why it was done.

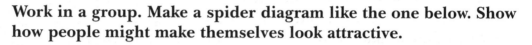

> When a Chinese girl was two, her mother would …
>
> The Chinese thought small feet were … If a woman had large feet when she got married …

3.6 Work in a group. Make a spider diagram like the one below. Show how people might make themselves look attractive.

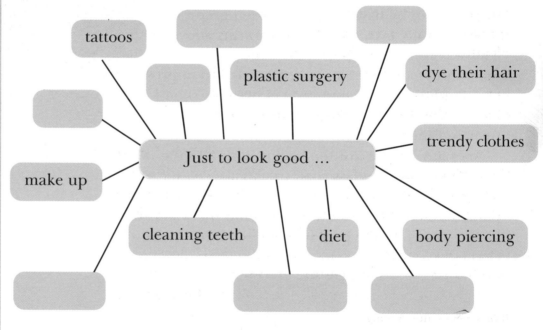

tattoos

plastic surgery

dye their hair

trendy clothes

Just to look good …

make up

cleaning teeth   diet   body piercing

3.7

SKILLS
PAGE 21

Work in small groups. Sort the above ideas into what you think is reasonable and unreasonable. Give your reasons. Hold a class debate, using the following points of view:

> People should do what they like to look good.

> You can go too far trying to look good.

Wild Swans

My grandmother's feet had been bound when she was two years old. Her mother, who herself had bound feet, first wound a piece of white cloth about **twenty feet** long
5 round her feet, bending all the toes except the big toe inward and under the sole. Then she placed a large stone on top to crush the arch. My grandmother screamed in agony and begged her to stop. Her mother had to
10 stick a cloth into her mouth to gag her. My grandmother passed out repeatedly from the pain.

    The process lasted several years. Even after the bones had been broken, the feet
15 had to be bound every day and night in a thick cloth because the moment they were released they would try to recover. For years my grandmother lived in **relentless, excruciating** pain. When she
20 pleaded with her mother to untie the bindings, her mother would weep and tell her that unbound feet would ruin her entire life, and that she was doing it for her own future happiness.

25   In those days, when a woman was married, the first thing the bridegroom's family did was to **examine** her feet. Large feet, meaning normal feet, were considered to bring shame on the husband's household. The mother-in-law would lift the hem of the bride's long skirt, and if her feet were more
30 than about four inches long, she would throw down the skirt in a **demonstrative gesture of contempt** and stalk off, leaving the bride to the critical gaze of the wedding guests.

Wild Swans by Jung Chang

twenty feet – about six metres

relentless, excruciating – terrible

examine – look at

demonstrative gesture of contempt – in disgust

3.8 Read the poem opposite. Which sentence describes each stanza best?

1 The poet is saying why he wants the trainers.

2 The poet is saying what the trainers will do for him.

3 The poet is describing what the trainers are like.

3.9 Work in a group. Practise reading the poem. Look at the ideas below. You could make a tape recording to play to the rest of the class.

1 Choose some lines to read singly, in pairs or as a group.

2 Make some lines quicker or quieter, louder or slower.

3 Work out which words you want to stand out.

4 Choose some sound effects to add.

3.10 Choose the five lines in the poem which you like best. Explain why you chose each of them.

3.11

TRF
PAGE 21

Write a television script to advertise the trainers. Use the five lines you chose. Draw or describe the picture (shot) the camera will show with each line.

You could start your advertisement like this.

Shot 1 A trendy group of teenagers are playing football in a park. As a boy approaches, all eyes turn to his feet.

VOICEOVER: Trainers ... that magnetize the eyes of your mates ...

I Want Trainers

that stand out in a crowd,
that mark you number one on the block,
that raise you off the concrete,
that **stamp your identity** on the streets,
5   that make your every footstep a dance,
that find their own way through town,
that **magnetize** the eyes of your mates,

with innersoles like trampolines
with tongues that reach your knees
10   with laces that hang loose,
with gold-plated lettering,
with treads deeper than tractor wheels,
with footprints that spell danger,
with hugely **inflated price-tags**

15   because the way I am I'm a **nonentity**,
because even Sam has got a pair,
because you love me and you're my parents,
because feet need all the attention they can get,
because I'm suffering severe shoe envy,
20   because what I wear is what I am,
because if I don't get them I might as well be DEAD!

By Norman Silver

stamp your identity – show what kind of person you are

magnetize – people's eyes are pulled towards the trainers

inflated price-tags – the prices are much too high

nonentity – someone who is not noticed

Adjectives

Read the two advertisements below.

> **1** Make a list of the words that describe the hair in advertisement A.
>
> **2** Make a list of the words that describe the hair in advertisement B.
>
> **3** Which shampoo will people want to buy? Why?

A

Do you dream of dull, greasy, tangled hair?
Use Rock shampoo and your dream
will come true.

B

Do you dream of shiny, clean, attractive hair?
Use Rock shampoo and your dream
will come true.

SKILLS

PAGE 26

SEE ALSO

PAGE 22

The words you chose in your answers above are **adjectives**. They are often called 'describing words'.

An adjective describes a noun. It makes your writing exciting and interesting.

He brushed his hair.
↑
noun

He brushed his rugged, dark, spiky hair.
↑ ↑ ↑
adjectives

3.13

TRF
PAGE 22

SKILLS
PAGES 25–26

Finish this advertisement for ZAP spot cream. Choose from the adjectives below.

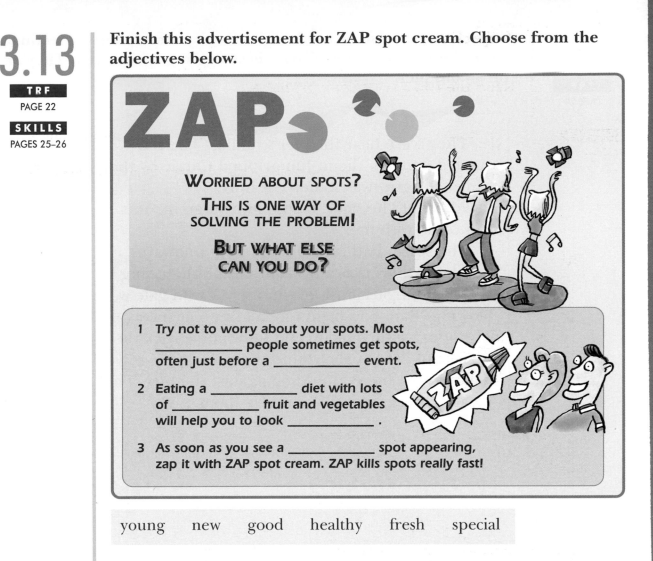

ZAP

WORRIED ABOUT SPOTS?

THIS IS ONE WAY OF SOLVING THE PROBLEM!

BUT WHAT ELSE CAN YOU DO?

1 Try not to worry about your spots. Most _____ people sometimes get spots, often just before a _____ event.

2 Eating a _____ diet with lots of _____ fruit and vegetables will help you to look _____ .

3 As soon as you see a _____ spot appearing, zap it with ZAP spot cream. ZAP kills spots really fast!

young	new	good	healthy	fresh	special

3.14

Work in pairs. Make notes for an advertisement for a new brand of toothpaste. Answer these questions.

Use adjectives from the box in some of your answers. Think of some others that will make people want to buy your toothpaste.

1 What is the toothpaste called?

2 What does it taste like?

3 What does it do to your teeth?

4 What does it do to your 'image'?

fresh	clean	bright
shiny	minty	tingling
dazzling	cool	healthy
attractive	good-looking	

3.15

Now write your advertisement. Use the adjectives you chose.

Adjectives can also be used to give a story atmosphere or feeling. Read the passage below. Carrie is struggling against Jim. They are on an old pier.

> They were near the pier's railing. The sea swirled beneath them. Jim gripped Carrie by the arms. His grip was so fierce it hurt.
>
> 'All right,' he said. 'If I go in, you go in. You can come with me.'
>
> The storm had crept up on them unawares. Suddenly there was a brilliant flash of lightning and a disastrous crash of thunder. A wild gale was blowing. Rain had begun to fall in great sheets. Thunder crashed again and lightning struck the surface of the sea all around them. Now the waves had become huge, thudding against the pier. The pier itself began to shake under them.

Adapted from *Hall of Mirrors* by Phil Preece

3.17 **Choose four adjectives from the passage that make the weather seem really powerful. Write them down.**

3.18 **Now read this description of Jim. How do you feel about him? Which adjectives make you feel that way?**

> Jim's head was thrown back. For one awful moment she saw his face fixed in a terrible grin. His dead hands tightened their bony grip on Carrie's arm and her heart grew cold in her body.

3.19

Work in pairs. First look carefully at these pictures. Then answer the questions below.

3.20

Work out several different ways the story could end. Use the questions below to help you. Choose the best idea. Then plan your ending.

1 How could Carrie escape?

2 Could someone rescue her? Who?

3 Could something happen to Jim to stop him hurting her?

3.21

PAGE 27

On your own, write a short ending. Include some vivid adjectives. Use the text below to get started. Fill in the gaps with adjectives from the box.

A _____ _____ flash of lightning hit the pier and Carrie could see the _____ railing. She was so near. Only another few feet and she would topple into the _____ _____ sea below.

deep black   broken   bright jagged

It's a mystery

4.1 Herculeah's mother is a detective. Read the passage opposite about her new client. Answer the questions below.

4.2 Write down the phrases in the text which prove the sentences below are true.

1 The man's size is scary (lines 7–9).

2 The man is behaving suspiciously (lines 10–18).

3 The man is like an animal (lines 11–13).

4 Herculeah's mother feels afraid (lines 1–4, 23–28).

4.3

SKILLS

PAGES 28–29

Invent another scary client. Follow the plan below to start your writing. Use some of the adjectives in the box and add your own.

1 Give the client a name.

2 Say how the client moves when entering the room.

... rushed in like a spider running across a web.

3 Describe the face in detail.

4 Describe what the client is wearing.

5 Describe the client's voice saying 'Good morning'.

> **movements:** slow, quick, spider-like, awkward, fierce
> **face:** piercing, sharp, thin, cold, cruel
> **clothes:** long, short, dark, neat, flowing, greasy, tattered
> **voice:** rough, mumbled, rushed, loud, quiet, shrill, low

The Dark Stairs

Her mother was at her desk. Her hands were stretched out in front of her. She was gripping a letter opener as if she was going to use it as a weapon.

5   The client was not seated. He stood facing the desk. His back was towards Herculeah.

Herculeah drew in her breath at the size of the man. He was huge.

He was more than huge. The man was a giant.
10 His shoulders were **hunched** forward, as if to make himself less noticeable. At the end of his long, ape-like arms were hands in black leather gloves.

The man still wore his overcoat. His hat was
15 pulled down low over his forehead.

Herculeah couldn't see his face. She thought there was something **suspicious** about the way he deliberately kept it turned away.

'Oh, I didn't know you had a client,' Herculeah
20 said politely. She was surprised that her voice sounded normal. 'I just wanted to tell you about some glasses I tried on. It can wait.'

'If it's important, I can take a break.'

'No.'

25 Herculeah paused. Did her mother want to, as she put it, take a break? Her mother had never suggested such a thing before. Clients came first with her mum.

Adapted from *The Dark Stairs:*
A Herculeah Jones Mystery by Betsy Byars

hunched – bent over

suspicious – makes you feel something is wrong

4.4

The poem opposite is a ballad (a poem that tells a story). A child is asking what has happened to his older sister. Each verse has a clue in it. Read the poem. Then answer the questions below.

4.5

Work in pairs. Put these pictures in the same order as the stanzas in the poem.

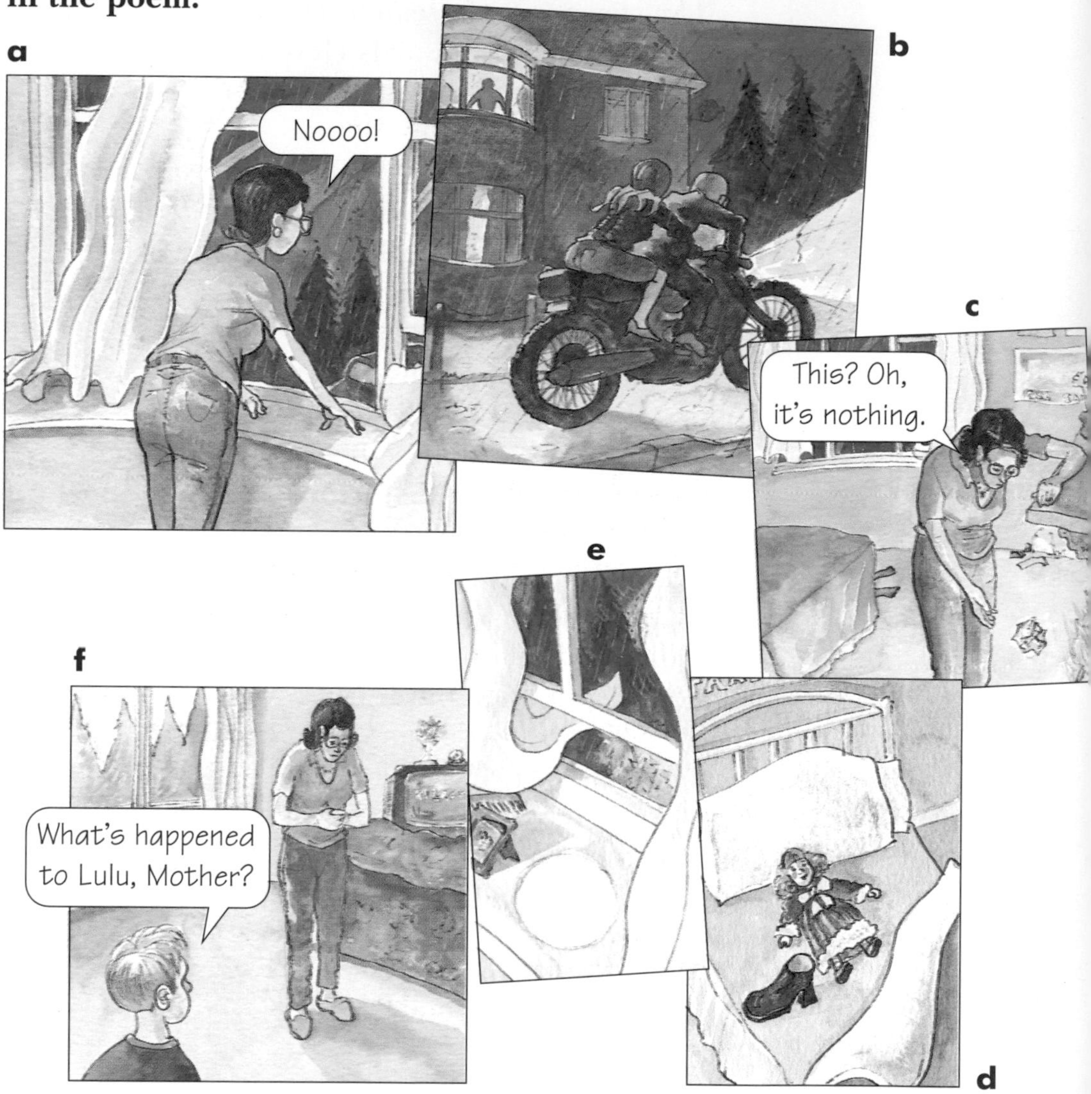

4.6

SKILLS
PAGE 31

Work in pairs. Use the poem and pictures. Work out the story that Lulu's brother would tell about what happened to Lulu last night.

Last night when everyone was asleep my sister Lulu …

4.7

TRF
PAGE 25

Work on your own. Write a diary entry for Lulu's brother. He is explaining what happened when Lulu disappeared.

What Has Happened to Lulu?

What has happened to Lulu, mother?
    What has happened to Lu?
There's nothing in her bed but an old rag doll
    And by its side a shoe.

5   Why is her window wide, mother,
    The curtain flapping free,
And only a circle on the dusty shelf
    Where her money-box used to be?

Why do you turn your head, mother,
10   And why do the tear-drops fall?
And why do you crumple that note on the fire
    And say it is nothing at all?

I woke to hear voices late last night,
    I heard an engine roar,
15 Why do you tell me the things I heard
    Were a dream and nothing more?

I heard somebody cry, mother,
    In anger or in pain,
But now I ask you why, mother,
20   You say it was a gust of rain.

Why do you wander about as though
    You don't know what to do?
What has happened to Lulu, mother?
    What has happened to Lu?

By Charles Causley

4.8 Read the newspaper article opposite. Then answer the questions below in as much detail as you can.

1 Read lines 1–23. What were Tom Smith and Co. asked to do?

2 What do we know about the young man?

3 Read lines 24–37. Why did the lady never write back to him?

4 Read lines 38–55. Why are the firm unable to find the lady now?

4.9
TRF
PAGE 26

Work in pairs. Imagine you knew what really happened. You are going to write to the *Daily Mail*. First make up your story by answering these questions.

1 How might the ring have got lost? Did someone at Tom Smith and Co. hide the ring on purpose? If so, why?

2 Do you think MM ever found out the ring had not arrived?

3 Do you think Miss Davies: *a)* knew MM was in love with her; *b)* wanted to marry MM; *c)* married someone else; *d)* stayed unmarried? Make up reasons to show why.

4 Do you think MM: *a)* never saw Miss Davies again; *b)* asked her to marry him again; *c)* married someone else; *d)* stayed unmarried? Make up what you think happened.

4.10
TRF
PAGE 26

Use your ideas to write a letter to the *Daily Mail* about what happened. Start like this.

Your address
Today's date

Dear Sir or Madam

I was interested to read ... This is what really happened ...

A cracker of a ring, but 70 years too late

SEVENTY years ago on Christmas Eve a young man waited **anxiously** to find out if his sweetheart would marry him. He had written to Tom Smith and Co., a famous maker of Christmas crackers. He had sent them ten **shillings** and a valuable diamond engagement ring.

He signed himself MM and only gave Chatham, Kent as his address. He asked them to put the ring, 'in one of your large crackers with the usual assorted odds and ends'. He asked the company to send the cracker to Miss W. Davies at her home in Rochester (Kent). He explained that it might cause a problem for the lady if he wrote himself.

Without a doubt MM hoped that Miss Davies would find the ring and write back to say she would be his bride. Sadly, he never heard from her. He must have thought that she did not want to marry him.

The truth was that the cracker had not been sent. The letter and the ring got lost in the London offices of the company. They were only found recently when an old safe was cleared out.

The token of a long-lost love

Staff tried hard to find the pair. The young lady's address was the Red House in Frindsbury Hill, Rochester. It was knocked down long ago to make way for new houses. Nobody in the area can remember her family.

'This is such a sad story,' said John Ford, a director of Tom Smith and Co. 'Both the lady and the gentleman are probably dead now, or must be nearly 100. The ring is quite valuable so he must have been quite a wealthy young man. We'll probably never know exactly what happened.'

Can you help solve the mystery? If so, write to the *Daily Mail*.

anxiously – he was feeling nervous, waiting for her answer
shilling – an old coin

Adapted from *Daily Mail*, 24 December 1997

4.11

SKILLS

PAGES 32–33

Read the newspaper article opposite. Look at how it is written and laid out.

Now write down the answers to these questions. They will give you a set of rules for writing a newspaper article. Look again at the opposite page to help you.

1 What should a headline do?

2 What is in the first paragraph of the article?

3 Which questions are answered by a newspaper article?

4 What adds interest to an article?

5 How is the text laid out on the page?

6 What is put under a photograph?

4.12

TRF

PAGE 27

Write a newspaper article based on the notes below. They are from a reporter's notebook. Use the set of rules to help you.

- Idea for headline: Slippery stowaway.

- Mrs Nissa Singh and family of 23 Cherry Road, Thame, returned from a holiday in Australia on Monday 21 May.

- Sunil, her 11-year-old son, saw his bag moving in his bedroom that night – 'It was really scary.'

- Nissa Singh – 'I thought Sunil was joking at first. Then I saw his bag move across the carpet, so I phoned the police.'

The three-metre python

- Police found that a three-metre baby python had hidden itself inside the bag. Police spokesman said, 'It's very unusual.'

- RSPCA will pass the baby python on to a zoo. 'It will be well looked after there.'

Thieves don't take the biscuit!

Thieves left £5000 worth of jewellery behind.

A PAIR OF THIEVES broke into a house yesterday but didn't find jewellery worth £5000 hidden in a biscuit tin!

Two robbers broke into the home of Mrs Eileen Tate, 39-year-old mother of two, of 14 Dolphin Way yesterday afternoon and ransacked the house. They took a CD player and a television set.

'Fortunately they didn't bother to look in the biscuit tin. That's where I'd hidden all my jewellery!' said Mrs Tate.

Police are appealing for witnesses. If you saw two men near Dolphin Way wearing jeans and denim jackets and carrying a CD player and television set, please contact Kent CID.

Prepositions

Find out about prepositions and solve a mystery too! Copy out and complete the passage. Choose words from the box.

The moon was hidden _____ the clouds. A cold wind was blowing rain _____ the trees. A key had been hidden _____ the doormat _____ the day. The thief tried the key _____ the lock and opened the door. The thief walked _____ the house and crept _____ the hallway.

behind   through   under   inside
during   in   beneath   into   over
above   along   on   underneath

The words you used all described where or when something *was*:

A key had been hidden <u>under</u> *the doormat* <u>during</u> *the day.*

Words which do this are called **prepositions**.

4.14

The thief is looking for a diamond ring. Write down four places where it might be. Use a different preposition each time. Underline your prepositions.

The ring might be <u>inside</u> the box.

The thief took the diamond ring and walked from 19 Queen's Road to a house on Jubilee Way. Describe the route the thief took. Underline the prepositions.

The thief left the house and walked <u>along</u> …

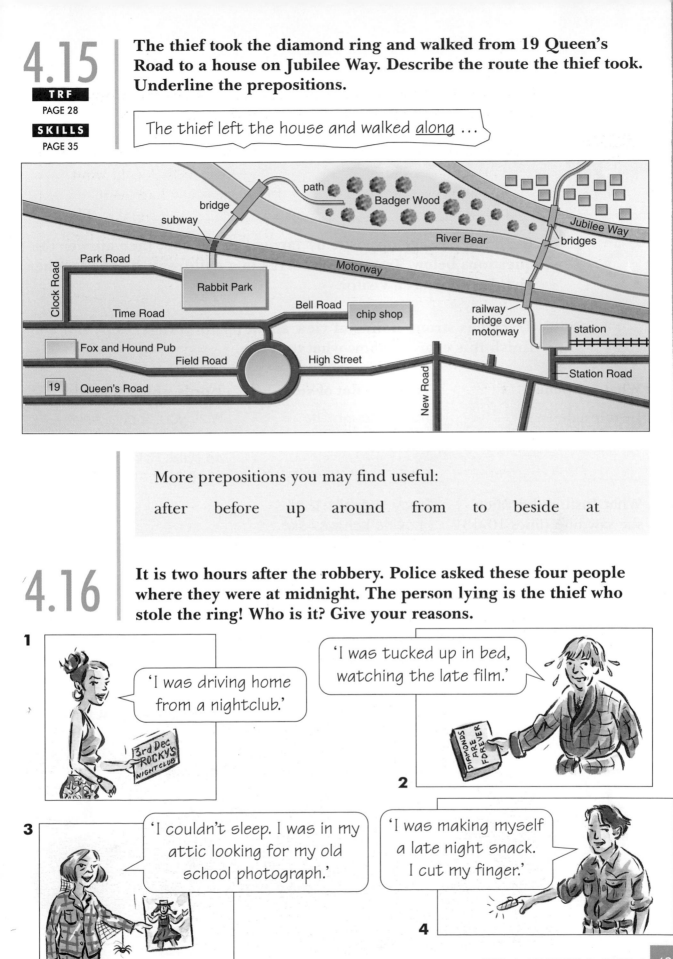

More prepositions you may find useful:

after   before   up   around   from   to   beside   at

4.16 **It is two hours after the robbery. Police asked these four people where they were at midnight. The person lying is the thief who stole the ring! Who is it? Give your reasons.**

1

'I was driving home from a nightclub.'

3rd Dec ROCKY'S NIGHTCLUB

'I was tucked up in bed, watching the late film.'

DIAMONDS ARE FOREVER

2

3

'I couldn't sleep. I was in my attic looking for my old school photograph.'

'I was making myself a late night snack. I cut my finger.'

4

Meet Jacqueline Wilson

5.1 Read the passage opposite by Jacqueline Wilson, then answer the questions below. Tracy Beaker lives in a children's home. Another girl, Justine, has a visitor.

5.2 Tracy has strong points of view about lots of things. Copy out and finish this chart to show what they are.

What happened	Tracy's point of view	Words which show this
Justine's dad arrived (lines 1–9)	Tracy thought he looked really silly.	Well, you should have seen him. Starting to go bald. Pot belly. Medallion.
What Justine did when she saw him (lines 10–13)	Tracy thought that Justine behaved like …	
How Tracy treated Justine (lines 17–21)	Tracy felt … so she …	
Justine cried (lines 21–28)	Tracy was … she never …	
Louise said Tracy was jealous (lines 29–36)	Again, Tracy was … and thought …	

5.3 Work in a group. Think about the whole passage. Do you think Tracy was jealous of Justine? Why?

5.4

SKILLS
PAGES 36–37

Write a description of Tracy Beaker. Use this plan.

Tracy is a girl who lives …
She has strong opinions about lots of things. She thinks …
Tracy can be mean. She was nasty to Justine when she …
Tracy acts as though she is 'hard', but … because …

The Story of Tracy Beaker

The next day Justine's famous dad put in an appearance at long last. Justine had gone on and on about how good-looking he was, just like a pop star. Actually he had an evening job

5 singing in pubs. This was why he couldn't be at home to look after her and her brothers. Well, you should have seen him. Starting to go bald. Pot belly. Medallion. He wasn't *quite* wearing a frilly shirt and flares, but almost.

10 You wouldn't catch me wanting a dad like that. But Justine gave a weird little whoop when she saw him. She jumped up into his arms like a great big baby. He took her on some dumb outing and when she got back

15 she was all bubbly and bouncy and showing off this … this present he'd bought her.

I don't know why, but I felt really narked at Justine. It was all right when she didn't get a visit, like us lot. But now I kept picking on

20 her and saying silly sniggery things about her dad. And then she burst into tears.

I was a bit shocked. I didn't say anything *that* bad. And I never thought a really tough girl like Justine would ever cry. *I* don't ever

25 cry, no matter what. I mean, my mum hasn't managed to come and visit me for ages. I don't even *have* a dad, but you won't catch me crying.

Then I got another shock. My friend

30 Louise turned on me.

'You are horrid, Tracy,' she said. Then she put her arms right round Justine and gave her a big hug. 'Don't take any notice of her. She's just jealous.'

35 Me, jealous? Of Justine? Of Justine's dopey dumb dad? She had to be joking.

Adapted from *The Story of Tracy Beaker* by Jacqueline Wilson

5.5 A student enjoyed *The Story of Tracy Beaker* by Jacqueline Wilson. Read the transcript (what he said) opposite.

5.6 Work in pairs. Look at how Mark's words are written down exactly as he said them.

1 Read lines 1–8. Write down an example of Mark repeating himself.

2 Read lines 9–17 and the key.

- Which punctuation marks show that Mark is pausing?

- Which speech shows that Mark does not always speak in whole sentences?

3 Read from line 18 to the end. Which word does Mark say when he hesitates?

5.7

SKILLS

PAGES 38–40

Now read what Mark wrote about the book, below. It contains what he said in lines 19–25 opposite.

Tracy lived in a children's home. A writer called Cam visited them. She grew to like Tracy and took her to McDonald's. They had a wonderful time. She also gave her a birthday cake and a pen.

5.8 A student started making notes about the difference between spoken and written language. He looked at lines 19–25 opposite and the passage above. Copy the table and finish his notes.

Features	Spoken language	Written language
1 Number of sentences	Mark doesn't always speak in …	Mark breaks his writing into …
2 Repeating himself	Mark repeats himself when he says …	Mark never…
3 Pausing	Mark pauses as shown by an a total of … He says 'erm' a total of …	Mark's writing flows and he never …
4 Past or present tense	Mark uses the present tense. For example, he says 'Tracy lives' and …	Mark uses the past tense. For example, he says 'Tracy lived' and …
5 Formal/informal language	Mark uses informal language. For example, he says Cam thinks Tracy's 'OK' and …	Mark uses formal language. For example, instead of saying Cam thinks Tracy's 'OK' he says… and …

MARK: I'd just like to say … I'd just like to say it was brilliant … I really enjoyed the story.

TEACHER: What made it so good?

5 MARK: Tracy Beaker … she's really naughty and funny … erm … She lives in a home because her mum left her there … she's always saying her mum's going to come and get her but she never does.

TEACHER: Does Tracy have any friends?

10 MARK: Not really … she used to have a friend called … called … I can't remember …

TEACHER: Louise?

MARK: Yes … but Louise has gone off with Justine so Tracy breaks her – I mean Justine's – 15 clock. There's a boy called Peter who wants to be Tracy's friend but Tracy doesn't like him … he's younger than her.

TEACHER: What happens in the story?

MARK: Tracy lives in this home … erm … then 20 some writer … some writer called Cam comes to see them and in the end she thinks Tracy's OK and takes her out … they go to McDonald's and it's brill … she gets Tracy a birthday cake … and … erm … she 25 gives her a pen.

TEACHER: Did you like the ending of the story?

MARK: Yes … because you think Cam is going to adopt Tracy and she's really nice … and … erm … Tracy really likes her.

Key

… a pause (the name for … is **ellipsis**)

47

5.9 Read the information opposite about Jacqueline Wilson, the author of *The Story of Tracy Beaker*.

5.10 Work in pairs. Make up a quiz of ten questions about Jacqueline Wilson. The answers must be in the passage. Try your quiz out on another pair.

5.11 Imagine that Jacqueline Wilson is coming to your school. In pairs, make a draft of a handout to persuade students to come to listen to her.

PAGE 30

1 Think of a heading that will grab people's attention.

2 Show where you will put a picture of Jacqueline Wilson.

3 Use your quiz questions and answers to help you:

- *explain who Jacqueline Wilson is and what she does*

- *choose some information from the passage that teenagers will find interesting.*

4 Invite people to listen to the author after school on a Tuesday. Write this in larger print.

5.12 Work with another pair. Read each other's handouts. What could each pair do to make them even better?

5.13 Make a final version of the handout. You may want to use a computer to make it look like a real handout.

Jacqueline Wilson

Jacqueline Wilson was born in Bath in 1945, but spent most of her childhood in Kingston-on-Thames. She always wanted to be a writer. As she grew up, she filled lots of Woolworth's exercise
5 books with stories. She worked first for a publisher. After she had an article published in *Jackie* magazine, she became a journalist in Scotland. She married at 19 and had a daughter, Emma, when she was 21. She's been writing books ever
10 since, and they have won lots of prizes!

Jacqueline's biggest passion – and her worst habit – is buying books. She has over 10 000 books crammed into every corner of her small house – and they've started to creep across the carpets.
15 She hates housework and cooking, but she doesn't have a washing machine because she likes doing her own washing by hand!

We asked Jacqueline Wilson:

What was your favourite subject
20 ### at school?
I liked English – writing compositions. I loved art, too, although it was hard to be any good with school poster paints and nearly bald brushes. I was useless
25 at maths and I hated PE.

What would you take to a
desert island?
As many books as I could carry; a portable CD player so I could listen
30 to my entire Queen collection every day; a fat notebook and a few pens.

What would you be glad to
leave behind?
The telephone – but I'd love to train
35 a seagull or two to deliver letters.

Verbs and verb phrases

5.14

Read this passage. Write out lines 5–10. Fill in the spaces using words from the box below.

Jacqueline Wilson loves buying (and reading!) books. What do you do in your spare time? Some people just flop on the sofa watching television and guzzling crisps and chocolate. Others want to do something more active.
They may _____ sport, _____ their bikes,   5
_____ up with friends or even _____ a
mountain. Do you _____ lots of exercise? Or would
you rather watch a good match on television and
_____ that it is you out there? Which sort of
person _____you?   10

are	meet	climb	enjoy	have	imagine	ride

Each of the words you chose from the box is a **verb**.
Verbs tell you what someone is:

feeling	She **enjoys** sport.
doing	He **climbs** mountains.
having	He **has** lots of exercise.
thinking	He **imagines** shooting the winning goal.
being	Which sort of person **are** you?

5.15

Work in pairs. Which words in bold are verbs?

I **enjoy** listening to the **radio**. I **listen** to Radio 1 most of all. I **think** it's the best! They **have** a really good range of **music** and the DJs are great fun. I usually **phone** up to enter the competitions, but usually the lines **are** busy or I am too late. **Once** I did get through. Even though I did not win, they **played** a record for me.

TRF
PAGE 31

Not all verbs are single words. Read the paragraph below. Each sentence contains a **verb phrase** made up of more than one word. It is written in bold.

> I **will go** to town on Saturday. I **might go** with some friends, but if they are busy I **will have to go** by myself. I **can spend** hours trying on clothes even if I **have** not **got** any cash. Then when I **do have** some money, I know what to buy!

Each of the verb phrases above has a **main** verb.

will **go**   **will** go

↑   ↑

main verb: **go**: the main thing being done

auxiliary verb: **will**: auxiliary means 'helping'. Words such as **should**, **used to**, **has** and **will** help the main verb to do its job.

5.16

Now read the sentences below. Find and write down the verb phrase in each one.

1 I should do some exercise.

2 I used to go swimming twice a week with Salman.

3 He has joined a band now.

4 I will buy myself a new swimsuit.

5 Perhaps Misha will come instead.

5.17

PAGE 42

Make a chart showing the main and auxiliary verbs in each of the verb phrases you noted above.

Verb phrase	Auxiliary (helping) verb	Main verb
should do	should	do

Verb tenses

The events in the passages on this page take place at different times. The verbs have to be in the right **tense** to show this.

1 Passage A is written in the **present tense** – things are happening now: *I **have** lots of books.*

2 Passage B is written in the **past tense** – things have already happened: *I **watched** lots of sport …*

3 Passage C is written in the **future tense** – things are going to happen: This weekend *I **will go** to Alton Towers …*

5.18

Three students are saying what they enjoy in their spare time. Read the passages. Copy out the last two sentences of each passage. Fill in the blanks with words from the box.

| smashed | are | will be | broke | are | will go | enjoy |

A

I have lots of books. Jacqueline Wilson is my favourite author. I think her best book is *Double Act*. I _____ her books because they _____ really funny. The characters _____ really lively too.

B

I watched lots of sport over the weekend. England beat France in the rugby. It was a really exciting match. Then I saw the Grand Prix. One of the cars _____ into another car and then carried on racing. The driver _____ his arm in the crash, but he still went on to win the race.

C

This weekend I will go to Alton Towers with the youth group. We will catch the coach at seven o'clock. I _____ _____ on all the rides I can – especially *Nemesis*. We _____ _____ back at about ten o'clock in the evening.

5.19

What tense are each of these sentences in: present, past or future? List the verbs that show this.

1 Our hundredth school fête will take place on Saturday.

2 Everyone will dress up in Victorian costumes.

3 I am excited about it.

4 Last year there were lots of different stalls.

5 I won a Game Boy in the raffle.

5.20

SKILLS
PAGE 43

Write three sentences about the picture below in this order.

1 Write a sentence in the present tense.

2 Write a sentence in the past tense.

3 Write a sentence in the future tense.

The past tense is often used to write stories, reports and diary entries:

Tracy ran down the stairs. The letter Elaine was holding had to be for her. Had her mother finally written to her?

The present tense is often used to write stage directions for plays:
Tracy is running down the stairs. Elaine is holding out a white envelope.

All abroad!

6.1 Read the West Indian folk tale opposite. It was written for younger children. Anansi the spider has been told to catch Snake and take him to Tiger. Stop at a question in a box. Answer it before you read on.

6.2 Which parts of the story show that each of these opinions is true?

> **1** Anansi is very clever.

> **2** Snake is very proud of his length.

6.3

TRF
PAGES 34–35

Work in pairs. Plan an ending to the story that younger children will find fun and easy to follow.

1 What will Anansi say to trick Snake to have the rest of his body tied to the bamboo?

2 Where will Anansi take Snake now he is tied up? What might Snake say when he realises he's been tricked? How might Anansi feel?

3 Anansi has won his bet. What might Tiger give Anansi as a reward?

6.4 You are going to tell your story on television in a new programme for 5–7-year-olds.

Practise the story and either:
- video it
- tell it in small groups
- tell it to a younger class.

Voices
Make it fun – try giving the animals different voices. Remember that:
- Anansi is clever
- Snake is proud.

What could you use as visual aids?

Children like to see actions as well as hear a voice.

'I had a bet with Tiger,' said Anansi the spider. 'I told him you are the longest animal in the world, longer even than that bamboo tree! But Tiger says that the bamboo tree is longer.'

5   At this Snake stretched himself out on the grass. 'Look!' he shouted. 'Look! How dare Tiger say that the bamboo tree is longer than I am!'

'Well,' said Anansi, 'you are very long indeed. But Snake, now you and the bamboo tree are near I can
10   see that the bamboo tree is just a few centimetres longer. I have lost my bet. Tiger wins!'

What do you think Snake will tell Anansi to do?

'Tiger, fiddlesticks!' shouted Snake. 'Anyone can see that stupid bamboo tree is shorter than I am. Cut it
15   down, you stupid creature! Put it beside me. Measure the bamboo tree against my body. You haven't lost your bet, you have won.'

Anansi hurried off to the clump of bamboos, cut down the longest and trimmed off the branches.
20   'Now lay it beside me,' shouted the impatient Snake.

Anansi put the long bamboo pole beside Snake. Then he said, 'Snake, you are very long indeed. But we must do this the correct way. Perhaps when I run up to your head you will crawl up, and when I run
25   down to your tail you will wriggle down. How I wish I had someone to help me measure you with the bamboo!'

What do you think Snake will suggest Anansi does now?

'Tie my tail to the bamboo,' said Snake, 'and get on
30   with the job.'

Adapted from *Tiger Story, Anansi Story* from *West Indian Folk Tales*
by Philip Schofield

6.5 Read the passage from a holiday brochure opposite. Then answer the questions below.

6.6 Work in pairs. How would each of the people below feel about a holiday in Jamaica? Why?

1 Hannah belongs to a climbing club. She loves mountains and beautiful scenery. She thinks sunbathing is boring.
Hannah would enjoy … because … However, she would not like …

2 Robert enjoys the hustle and bustle of big cities.

3 Jamila wants to stay in a top-class hotel. She wants to wind-surf.

6.7

SEE ALSO
PAGES 20–21

Work in pairs. Discuss how the brochure makes Jamaica sound like a great place to go on holiday. Start by looking for:

1 Five facts about the holiday in Jamaica.
1 Five-star hotels

2 Five descriptions that make Jamaica's landscape sound attractive. Underline the adjectives.
1 <u>Dazzling</u> <u>white</u> <u>sandy</u> beaches

6.8

TRF
PAGE 36

SKILLS
PAGES 44–45

SEE ALSO
PAGES 30–31

Write three paragraphs for a holiday brochure page. It should be about somewhere good for family holidays. Follow this plan.

1 Describe the place. Use adjectives that make it sound attractive.

2 Explain what there is to do on holiday. Include six facts.

3 Explain why it will suit parents, teenagers and children.

Adjectives you may like to use		Nouns you may like to use	
large	sandy	exciting	nightclub	playground
happy	lively	fun-packed	bar	swimming pool
trendy	safe	friendly	entertainment	television
			theme park	sun room
			babysitting service	

With five-star hotels, gorgeous beaches and all the nightlife you could wish for, this beautiful island is one of the world's top holiday resorts. 5

Jamaica

A favourite playground of the rich and famous since the 1920s, Jamaica is 10 one of the largest, **lushest** and most laid-back of all the Caribbean islands.

All around the coast are dazzling white sandy beaches and pretty sheltered coves. Each is gently washed by sparkling blue sea. You can relax and sunbathe or try every form of watersport from wind-surfing to **para-sailing**. In the evening you can dance the night away or take time to enjoy a luxurious meal. 15

Make time to explore the country's mountains and you'll find even more to appreciate. Jamaica has some of the Caribbean's most spectacular scenery. There are fast-flowing rivers, glittering streams, gushing waterfalls and, of course, the misty Blue Mountains where Jamaica's famous coffee is grown.

The island flows with the gentle rhythm of the **calypso** and **reggae** music. Life 20 is taken at a relaxed, unhurried pace. Jamaican people are so friendly and easy-going, their view is summed up in the simple catch-phrase, 'no problem', which you're bound to hear many times during your stay.

lushest – full of colour and beauty
para-sailing – a motor boat pulls someone along, who glides through the air with a parachute
calypso – West Indian song
reggae – West Indian music with a rhythmic beat

6.9 Read the poem opposite. The poet is describing her South African grandfather.

6.10 Work in pairs. Finish the sentences below which describe the grandfather.

1 You can tell the grandfather is very old. His face is … and his arms have … Even his voice is … (lines 1–9)

2 He carved … (three things) (lines 10–30)

3 Grandfather wears … (lines 19–22)

4 A present of … makes him smile. (lines 23–25)

5 Grandfather remembers … (four things) (lines 26–33)

6.11 Work in pairs. The poet describes her grandfather by saying he is *like* something else. She uses a *comparison*.

Discuss the comparisons in lines 3–4, 5–6, 12 and 20–21. Use a chart like the one below to record your findings.

Line	Comparison	How grandfather is like this
3–4	grandfather's face is scribbled like a little sister's sketch.	His face is full of lines and wrinkles, like a child's scribble.
5–6	his arms are …	

6.12 Write a poem. Think of a person you like a lot and describe them. Include five comparisons.

List five of that person's feature's (eyes, clothes …). For each feature decide what you can best compare it to. You can write your comparisons like this:

My friend has … like …
His/her hair is as … as …

Grandfather

my grandfather's eyes
are sea fog grey.
his face is scribbled
like a little sister's sketch,
5 his arms marked
like a giraffe.
my grandfather's voice
is a chirping bird
in a sunset nest
10 hands that carved **kraal** patterns
on boxes and bowls
shake like shivering children.
he carved this **whistle bird**
at the end of an **ox thong**
15 round my neck.
grandfather's smell
is **tobacco earth**
ripe for reaping.
he sits sun-trapped
20 in **pants** wide
like water pipes –
specials from the trading store.
and if you bring him
ten cents tobacco,
25 he'll smile a **crescent moon**,
and chirp a tale
of how he walked
ten miles to school,
carved a **kudu horn**
30 for **the Fathers**,
cried when granny died,
how as a young man
sun ripe, he saw the seasons.

By Dorian Haarhoff

traditional patterns

a type of flute

a leather string

ground where
tobacco grows

trousers

new moon

horn made from
a deer antler

the priests

Similes

Sometimes writers make a picture in words to help them describe something. This is called **imagery**. When the words **as** or **like** are used to compare things in an image, it is called a **simile**:

his face is scribbled **like a little sister's sketch**,

thing   *simile*

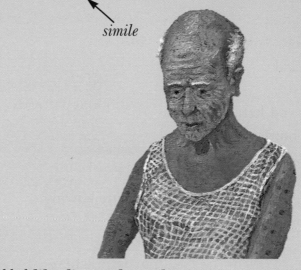

*The rain sparkled **like diamonds on the grass**.*
*The rainbow was **as thin as a ribbon**.*

6.13
TRF
PAGE 37

Work in pairs. Which of the descriptions below are similes?

1 Lightning flashed across the African sky.

2 The thunder sounded like a train.

3 I ran really fast.

4 Drops of rain pelted me like stones.

5 Splashes of mud clung to my jeans, as sticky as glue.

6.14
TRF
PAGE 37

Write down what was being compared in each simile.

The sound of thunder is being compared to ...

6.15

Copy out and complete these similes.

1 In the distance the market looked _____ a patchwork quilt.

2 The noise from it was as loud _____ a football crowd.

6.16

SKILLS
PAGE 46

Look at the pairs of objects below. Use them to write a simile describing each person.

1   The veins on his hand were twisted like tree roots.

2

3

6.17

Write a description of the market below. Include four similes. Think about:

1 The things for sale.   2 How people look.   3 What people are doing.

Sentences: subject and object

6.18

Which of these are sentences?

> 1 My friend went to the market.
>
> 2 I last Saturday.
>
> 3 Mr Smith said the market has the cheapest fruit.
>
> 4 Ten apples 50p.

TRF
PAGE 38
SKILLS
PAGE 48

A sentence must have a verb. The ones that were not sentences did not have a verb.

I last Saturday.   I **went** last Saturday.

This is not a sentence because it has no verb   *This is a sentence – **went** is the verb*

The **subject** of the sentence is the person or thing that *does* the verb:

Mr Smith **said** the market has the cheapest fruit.

Who said the market has the cheapest fruit? Mr Smith said it. Mr Smith is the subject of the sentence.

6.19

First list the verbs in these sentences.

> 1 I packed my bag quickly.
>
> 2 Our train went at ten o'clock.
>
> 3 Andy phoned for a taxi.
>
> 4 The taxi driver drove really quickly.

6.20

Now write down who or what is doing the verb in each sentence. That is the *subject* of the sentence.

6.21

TRF
PAGE 38

Now find the subject in each of the sentences below. The verbs are in bold.

1 At the station I **bought** a magazine.

2 We only just **caught** the train.

3 Andy **found** seats by the window.

4 Sue and Andy **drank** a can of coke.

5 Our friends **met** us in London.

SKILLS
PAGE 49

1 Many sentences have an **object**. The object is the person or thing a verb is done to:

Sue and Andy **drank** a can of coke.

↑
verb

Sue and Andy drank – what? **a can of coke**.
a can of coke is the object of the sentence.

Our friends **met** us in London.

Our friends met – who? **us**
us is the object of the sentence.

2 The object must answer the question **who?** or **what?** Something which answers the question **where?** or **when?** is not an object.

Andy went to London.

to London is not an object.

6.22

Look back to sentences 1–5 above. Write down the object of each sentence.

Take your chance

7.1

Read the poem opposite. A woman is telling her second husband how she murdered her first husband. Then say what order the pictures under the poem should be in.

7.2

Work in pairs. One of you is the woman. The other is a policeman who is interviewing her. Act out their conversation. Use the notes to help you, and make your own.

The policeman	The woman
1 What happened first?	1 When my husband came home, he was …
2 What did you …	2 I sewed …
3 Then what …	3 He woke up and …
4 Didn't anyone …	4 No, I took the …
5 So people thought …	5
6	6

7.3

TRF
PAGE 40

SKILLS
PAGES 50–51

Now write the policeman's report. It has to be formal and serious. It will be read in court. Include the information from your role play. Start like this:

Subject The suspected murder of Alan Jones by Edith Jones.

I visited Edith Jones at 46 Key Road, Maindy on (*write in today's date*).

She explained that on the 23rd July her husband, Alan Jones, had come home drunk. Once she was sure that he was asleep she took …

Her Second Husband Hears Her Story

'STILL, Dear, it is incredible to me
　　That here, alone,
You should have sewed him up until he died,
And in this very bed. I do not see
How you could do it, seeing what might **betide**.'　　　happen

'Well, he came home one midnight, **liquored deep** –　　　drunk
　　Worse than I'd known –
And lay down heavily, and soundly slept:
Then, desperate driven, I thought of it, to keep
Him from me when he woke. Being an **adept**　　　skilful

'With needle and thimble, as he snored, click-click
　　An hour I'd sewn,
Till, had he **roused**, he couldn't have moved from bed,　　　woken up
So tightly laced in sheet and quilt and **tick**　　　mattress
He lay. And in the morning he was dead.

'**Ere** people came I drew the stitches out,　　　Before
　　And thus **t'was** shown　　　it was
To be a **stroke**.' – 'It's a strange tale!' said he.　　　his heart stopped
'And this same bed?' – 'Yes, here it came about.'
'Well, it sounds strange – told here and now to me.

'Did you intend his death by your tight **lacing**?'　　　sewing
　　'O, that I cannot **own**.　　　say
I could not think of else that would **avail**　　　work
When he should wake up, and attempt embracing.' –
　　'Well, it's a **cool queer tale**!'　　　strange story

By Thomas Hardy

7.4

Read the play script on the opposite page.

Eliza sells flowers on the streets of London. She has gone to see Higgins. She wants him to teach her to speak better English (with good grammar and no slang), so she can get a better job.

7.5

SKILLS

PAGES 52–53

Work in pairs. Read the sentences in lines 2, 3, 12 and 20–21 out loud. Look at the underlined words. What should Eliza say instead of the underlined words so that her English is correct?

7.6

In this play Eliza learns to speak Standard English. Standard English should be used in formal situations. Read about what happened to Eliza below. Then answer the questions.

Eliza is on her way to sell flowers. She sees a large cart run someone over. She gets a doctor. Later she tells her story to:

a) a policeman who wanted her to be a witness

b) a friend who wanted to know what happened

c) her boss who wanted to know why she was late.

1 In which cases does Eliza need to use Standard English?

2 When is it all right for Eliza to use slang and be less formal?

7.7

Work in pairs. Take it in turns. Act out the three times Eliza talks about the accident. Start by deciding which opening to use for each one. Make notes about how you will continue it.

1 I was on my way to work when I saw a large cart ...

2 I had to help out at an accident on the way to work ...

3 You'll never guess what happened to me on the way ...

HIGGINS:	Be off with you: I don't want you.
ELIZA:	Don't you be so saucy. You <u>aint</u> heard what I come for yet. *(to Mrs Pearce, the housekeeper)* Did you tell him I <u>come</u> in a taxi?
MRS PEARCE:	Nonsense, girl! What do you think a gentleman like Mr Higgins cares what you came in?
ELIZA:	Oh, we are proud! He aint above giving lessons, not him. I heard him say so. If my money's not good enough I can go elsewhere.
HIGGINS:	Good enough for what?
ELIZA:	Good enough for you. Now you know, don't you. I'm coming to have lessons, I am. And to pay for 'em too, make no mistake.
HIGGINS:	Well!!! What do you expect me to say to you?
ELIZA:	Well, if you <u>was</u> a gentleman, you might ask me to sit down, I think. Don't I tell you I'm bringing you business?
HIGGINS:	*(to his friend Pickering)* Shall we ask this baggage to sit down or shall we throw her out of the window?
ELIZA:	I won't be called a baggage when I've offered to pay like any lady.
PICKERING:	But what is it you want?
ELIZA:	I want to be a lady in a flower shop 'stead of sellin' at the corner of Tottenham Court Road. But they won't take me unless I can talk more **genteel**. He said he could teach me. Well, here I am ready to pay him – not asking any favour – and he treats me <u>zif</u> I was dirt.

From *Pygmalion* by Bernard Shaw

genteel – lady-like

5 10 15 20

7.8 Read the passage opposite. Then answer the questions below. The *Titanic* was a huge ship. No one believed it could ever sink, but on 15 April 1912 it did. A fireman remembers what happened.

7.9 Work in pairs. Which sentence is true: *a)* or *b)*? Find the lines in the story which show you are right.

1 *a)* The *Titanic* sank because the boilers burst.
 b) The *Titanic* hit an iceberg and sank.

2 *a)* Firemen were allowed on any deck.
 b) Harry risked his life going to the hurricane deck.

3 *a)* Only the Italian mother and one baby died.
 b) Even the baby in Harry's arms was dead.

4 *a)* There was no room in the lifeboat, so the man hit Harry with the oar to keep him away.
 b) The man hit Harry with the oar by accident.

7.10 Work in pairs. Find eight facts which tell what happened when the *Titanic* sank. Record what you find using a flow chart.

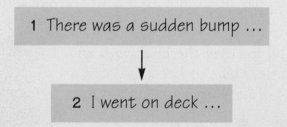

1 There was a sudden bump ...

2 I went on deck ...

7.11

TRF
PAGE 41

Harry Senior has to write a formal letter to the ship's owners about what happened. The work on page 70 will help you write the final letter. First make notes about the following.

1 What orders were given once the *Titanic* began sinking?

2 How did people try to help one another?

3 How and why did people die?

The Titanic

I was in a **bunk** when I felt a bump. One man said 'Hello. **She** has been struck.' I went on deck and saw a great pile of ice from the **iceberg** on the well deck, but we all thought the ship would last some time, and we went back to our bunks.

Then one of the firemen came running down and yelled, 'All **muster** for the lifeboats.' I ran on to the well deck, and the Captain said, 'All **firemen** keep down on the well deck. If a man comes up, I'll shoot him.'

Then I ran up on to the hurricane deck and helped to throw one of the **collapsible** boats on the lower deck. I saw an Italian woman holding two babies. I held one of them, and made the woman jump overboard with the baby, while I did the same with the other. When I came to the surface the baby in my arms was dead. I saw the woman begin to swim hard, but a boiler burst on the *Titanic* and started a big wave. Then, as the woman saw that wave, she gave up. Then, as the child was dead, I let it sink too.

I swam around for about half an hour, and was swimming on my back, when the *Titanic* went down. I tried to get aboard a lifeboat, but some chap hit me over the head with an oar. There were too many in her. I got around to the other side of the boat and climbed in.

Adapted from a report given by Harry Senior

5

10

15

20

25

bunk – bed
She – sailors talk about boats as if they are female
iceberg – floating mountain of ice
muster – gather
firemen – men who looked after the fire which powered the ship's engine
collapsible – folding

7.12

TRF
PAGE 41

SKILLS
PAGES 54–55

Look at how a formal letter is laid out, opposite. Then copy out and complete each rule below. Explain where each part of the letter goes on the page.

Rules to help you write a formal letter

1 The address of the person writing the letter goes ... Each part of the address goes on a new line: street, town, county, post code.

2 The date goes ...

3 Leave a line ...

4 The name and address of the person who is going to receive the letter go on the ...

5 The letter should begin *Dear Name* or *Dear Sir or Madam*.

6 The letter starts on the next ...

7 Use paragraphs to break up the text.

> In paragraph 1 use the information from the answer to question 1 of 7.11.
>
> In paragraph 2 use the information from the answer to question 2 of 7.11.
>
> In paragraph 3 use the information from the answer to question 3 of 7.11.

8 At the _____ of the letter the writer has to sign off. This goes on the _____ hand side of the page.

You should write
Yours faithfully if the letter began *Dear Sir or Madam*
Yours sincerely if the letter began *Dear Name*

9 The person's signature goes ... Then their name is printed below.

7.13

TRF
PAGE 41

Use these rules and your notes from page 68 to write the letter Harry Senior sent. You will get one mark for each rule you follow correctly.

1 56 Cliff Road
Dover
Kent
DR5 3BB
2 28 April 1912

3

4 Mr J. Bruce Ismay
Managing Director
White Star Line
Gold Street
London SW1

5 Dear Mr Ismay

6 This is my account of what I saw after the *Titanic* was struck by an iceberg ...

7
> **A formal letter should be serious and polite. You should not be chatty or too friendly.**
>
> **The letter should be divided into paragraphs. Start a new paragraph for each new subject you write about.**

I hope that this makes clear what happened to me at that dreadful time.

8 Yours sincerely

9 *Harry Senior*

Harry Senior (Fireman)

7.14

Where does today's English language come from? In pairs, write a short quiz using the following information. Swap your quiz with another pair. Answer each other's questions.

For centuries people have travelled on ships. Travellers and invaders taught their language to people in the countries they visited. Until about the sixth century, most people in England spoke a language similar to Welsh or Cornish. The map shows who came to Britain and made a difference to the English language.

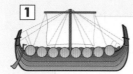

1

Angles and Saxons came from **North Europe** in the fifth and sixth centuries. Their local languages merged and became known as Anglo-Saxon:
England comes from **Angle-land.**
Gang comes from a word brought by the Angles and Saxons, **gangen**, meaning 'to go'. It was used of people who travelled in groups for safety.

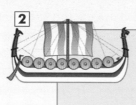

2

Christian missionaries came from the **Roman Empire** from about the third century onwards. They brought Latin and Greek words:
wine comes from the Latin word **vinum**
ball comes from the Greek word **ballo**, which means 'to throw'.

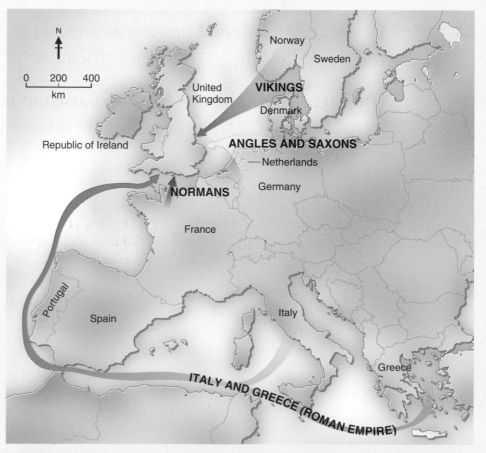

Words

vinegar came from the French words *vin aigre* meaning 'sour wine'. Wine left in the open for several days becomes bitter. Instead of wasting it, the French sprinkled some on their salads to improve the taste. It is now known in England as *vinegar*, although today only expensive vinegar is made from wine.

 burger came from the German word *hamburger*. A hamburger was a steak made of beef in Hamburg in Germany. English speakers later thought a hamburger must be made of ham. So when they made a steak out of minced beef, they called it a *beefburger*.

orange came from the Arabic word *naranj*. Over time *naranj* turned into *norange*. Then, instead of 'a norange' it became 'an orange'.

tomato came from the Mexican word *tomatl*. When the Spanish invaded Mexico in the sixteenth century, they took back tomatl plants to grow. They had difficulty saying the 'tl' at the end. Many Spanish words end in 'o', so the word changed and came into English as *tomato*.

3 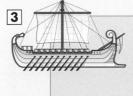 Vikings came from **Scandinavia** in the eighth century. They brought Old Norse words:
gold comes from the Old Norse word geld. The people in England had to pay taxes to the invaders and this was known as **Danegeld** – gold for the Danes.

4 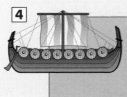 Normans came from **France** from 1066 onwards. They brought French words. The word sabotage comes from the French word sabot, which means '**wooden shoe**'. Sometimes French workers got fed up with their bosses. Then they would throw their wooden shoes into the machinery. This stopped it working. It became known as *sabot*aging.

Believe it or not!

8.1

SKILLS

PAGES 56–57

Read the passage on the opposite page. Then answer the questions below. Jerome is at boarding school while his father is abroad. His teacher has some bad news.

1 In your own words, explain what the story was about.

2 What did Jerome expect the teacher to say to him?

3 Did the ending of the story surprise you?

Graham Greene has used a **surprise ending** in this part of his story.

He made the reader expect one thing:
that Jerome's father had died a hero.

The end of the story was quite different:
Jerome's father was crushed by a pig.

8.2

TRF

PAGE 43

Turn the cartoon below into a story with a surprise ending. First work out a surprise ending. Then write your story.

I'm going to get Jerome.

Oh no, Mr Wordsworth.

Just who I hoped to bump into. Get my book from...

What will happen?

Who will get wet?

A Shocking Accident

'Sit down, Jerome,' Mr Wordsworth said. 'I've had a telephone call, Jerome. From your aunt. I'm afraid I have bad news for you.'

'Yes, sir?'

'Your father has had an accident.'

5   'Oh.'

Mr Wordsworth looked at him with some surprise. 'A serious accident.'

'Yes, sir?'

Jerome worshipped his father. He believed that
10 his father either '**ran guns**' or was a **member of the British Secret Service**. Now he wondered if his father had been wounded in a 'hail of machine-gun bullets'.

Mr Wordsworth played with the ruler on his desk.
15 He said, 'You know your father was in **Naples**?'

'Yes, sir.'

'Your aunt heard from the hospital today,' Mr Wordsworth said in desperation. 'It was a street accident.'

20   'Yes, sir?' It seemed quite likely to Jerome that they would call it a street accident. The police of course had fired first; his father would not kill except as a **last resort**.

'I'm afraid your father was very seriously hurt indeed.'
25   'Oh.'

'In fact, Jerome, he died yesterday. Quite without pain.'

'Did they shoot him through the heart?'

'I beg your pardon. What did you say, Jerome?'

'Did they shoot him through the heart?'

30   'Nobody shot him, Jerome. Your father was walking along a street in Naples when a pig fell on him. A shocking accident. In the poorer parts of Naples they keep pigs on their balconies. This one was on the fifth floor. It had grown too fat. The balcony
35 broke. The pig fell on your father.'

Adapted from *A Shocking Accident* by Graham Greene

ran guns – smuggled guns

member of the British Secret Service – spy

Naples – Italian city

last resort – final try

8.3 People thought the Russian royal family were all killed in 1918. Years later a woman called Anna said she had escaped and was the Russian Grand Duchess Anastasia. Read the information opposite.

8.4 Work in a group. Discuss these questions. Note down your answers.

1   What happened to the Russian royal family in 1918?

2   Who tested whether Anna was Anastasia? Find one person in passage A and two people in passage B.

3   Did Anna and Anastasia look similar? Find one comment in passage A and one comment in passage B.

4   Why did the following people in passage B not think Anna was Anastasia?
  - Pierre Gillard
  - Anastasia's aunt.

8.5

TRF
PAGE 44

Do you think Anna was Anastasia? Write a speech giving your reasons. Try to persuade people that you are right. Follow the plan below.

1   Explain what your point of view is.
  I think that Anna …   I don't think that Anna …

2   Use information from the text to explain *why* and *how* it shows you are right.
  For: Anna had blue eyes and looked a lot like ….
  Against: Anna would not speak Russian with …

8.6

TRF
PAGE 44

As a class, hold a debate on whether Anna is really Anastasia.

1   Listen to what people say that does not fit in with your point of view.

2   Come up with reasons to show why you think differently.

Although Anna had blue eyes and looked like Anastasia, she couldn't remember …

Anna may not have spoken Russian, but think about what the scientist said …

A Anna was Anastasia

Anna knew a lot about Anastasia's early life. She described how, in 1918, the family had been taken down to the cellar and shot and stabbed. Her own arms and legs were scarred and she had been shot in the head. Anna said she was the only member of the royal family found alive and described how someone had helped her to get away.

Anna looked a lot like the Grand Duchess Anastasia. She had the same blue eyes that Anastasia had inherited from her father. A scientist examined a photograph of Anastasia's face at seventeen and compared it with Anna's face. He said they were one and the same person.

Anastasia had a crooked finger. She damaged it by shutting it in a coach door. Anna's same finger was crooked too. Anna also had deformed feet – one was worse than the other. Anastasia had the same problem and it was the same foot that was worse.

Anastasia

B Anna was not Anastasia

In 1918 Anastasia was taken down to a cellar with the rest of the Russian royal family and shot and stabbed. Then soldiers were ordered to destroy all the bodies.

The woman called Anna spent a lot of time in a mental hospital before she claimed to be Anastasia. Anna would not speak any Russian with Anastasia's old teacher, Pierre Gillard, when he visited her. He said she did not remember many of the things that Anastasia would have known.

Anna would not talk to Anastasia's aunt. The aunt agreed that Anna looked like Anastasia, but said it was not her.

8.7 Read the story on the opposite page. It was first written by Chaucer in the fourteenth century. A writer has retold it in modern English.

8.8 Use your own words. Explain why Crow changed from a white, beautiful singing bird to a black bird with an ugly voice.

8.9 Work in pairs. Which of these best sums up the message in Crow's story? Give reasons.

1 A lie will always get you into trouble.

2 People do not always want to know the truth.

8.10 What do you think about telling the truth?

1 Do you think it is always best to tell the truth?

2 Can you think of any times when it might be 'right' to lie?

8.11

SKILLS
PAGE 58

Look at these three lines describing the crow taken from Chaucer's fourteenth-century version of the story.

> Whit was this crowe as is a snow-whit swan,
> Therwith in al this world no nyghtyngale
> Syngen so wonder myrily and weel.

1 Which of Chaucer's words mean the same as the ones in the chart? Copy the chart and write them in.

Today's English	Chaucer's English
white	whit
crow	
all	
nightingale	
'able to sing'	
merrily	
well	

2 Write Chaucer's three lines in modern English. You can change the order of the words so they make sense to a reader today.
The crow was as white as ...

Snowy Crow

You know Crow – blacker than a sack's inside. He was not always so. Once he was white. And his song flowed like honey. He sang in the court of Alexander and his Queen.

From his high **perch**, Crow saw everything. He saw the King ride off
5 to hunt. He saw the Queen – more beautiful than any – sit at her sewing.

So it was that he saw the Queen's lover call for a kiss and stay for a cuddle. He heard them speak of Love! Crow's feathers then grew colder than snow, and he huddled on the floor of his cage.

When King Alexander came home, he called out, 'Hello, Crow.
10 How went the day?' But Crow did not answer Alexander's greeting.

'How now, Crow? What's the matter?'

'Nothing – so long as I say nothing.' Crow's voice was cracked with crying.

'**Go to**, Crow. I *will* know.'

15 'Then know the Queen loves another far more than you.' And Crow's voice broke completely and was never mended.

The King's heart was filled like a **cauldron** with **scalding** anger. He drew his sword, and killed his Queen.

But even when she was dead, she was more beautiful than any living
20 woman. For twelve long hours the King thought. Then he spoke, 'Oh woe, Crow! You made me kill a lady more beautiful than any in the world. What made you lie?'

'I? Lie?'

'Yes. Lie! So, Crow, for ever more be blacker than the night to which
25 you have brought me!'

And as he spoke, the croaking Crow became ink-black and remained so forever.

Adapted from *The Canterbury Tales* by Geraldine McCaughrean

perch – seat
go to – come on
cauldron – cooking pot
scalding – extremely hot

Accent and dialect

8.12 **Read this passage. Mrs Hicks is offering to cook a poor family's Christmas turkey as they do not have an oven. The writer has tried to write down her words just as they sounded.**

'Now that's a bit of a difficulty, **aint** it? Tell **yer** what. **Ah'll** be cooking **me** own turkey on the morning, but there's a good fire going downstairs now. If **Ah** turn it to the oven you could cook **yers** now. It would be cooked **afore** midnight,
5 when **we goes** to bed. Yer could put some potatoes round, to bake, and **yer'd** have a **reet** good meal. **Yer** can put the pudding at the back **o' me** fire at the same time. Most **o'** the heat's only going up **t'**chimney.'

Adapted from *Twopence to Cross the Mersey* by Helen Forrester

People who speak English and live in different areas of Britain may sound quite different.
Some words may be pronounced differently. This is called **accent**.
*Mrs Hicks is from Liverpool. She says **Ah'll** instead of **I'll**.*

8.13 **How does Mrs Hicks say:**

1 you (in lines 1 and 6)?

2 right (in line 6)?

3 of (in line 7)?

4 the (in line 8)?

Mrs Hicks also uses some words and phrases that people from her area would say instead of Standard English words. This is called speaking in a **dialect**.
*She says **aint** instead of **isn't**.*

8.14

What does Mrs Hicks say instead of:

1 before (in line 4)?

2 we go (in line 5)?

3 my (in lines 2 and 7)?

8.15

Write down how Mrs Hicks would say these sentences in her accent and dialect. Change the words in bold. Look back at the passage opposite to help you.

1 Did **you** know **the** chimney **of my** house caught fire last night?

2 **Of** course we **go** to bed **before** ten o'clock, so we were asleep when it happened.

3 **You** know the fireman asked **my** Uncle if this was **the right** place, and there were flames on **the** roof!

8.16

SKILLS
PAGE 59

People in many television programmes speak with accents and dialects.

1 List the programmes you watch that use accents and dialects.

2 Collect as many different dialect words as you can. Make a list with their meanings.

3 Make a mini-dictionary of dialect words. Put the words in alphabetical order. Say what they mean and where they come from.

Dialect word	Meaning	Where it comes from
tatties	potatoes	Scotland

Prefixes, stems and suffixes

8.17

TRF

PAGES 45–46,
55–60

Many words can be broken into parts. Read the passage below. It describes a mysterious true event.

During the Second World War, hundreds of men **disappeared** without trace in Italy. One minute they were **marching** up a mountain. The top of the mountain was hidden by a cloud. A moment later they had **vanished**. More and more **foolish** soldiers **calmly** marched into the cloud. It seems **impossible**, but they never **reappeared**.

The words in bold are made up of several parts joined together.
If you look at the word **disappeared**, it is made from three parts:

1 **dis**	2 **appear**	3 **ed**
prefix	*stem*	*suffix*

dis comes *before* the word and is called a **prefix**.

A prefix changes the meaning of the stem.

dis + appear = **disappear**.

appear is the main or **stem** word

ed comes *after* the word and is called a **suffix**.

A suffix changes the way a word can be used:

appear + ed = **appeared**

8.18

Look back at the seven words in bold in the passage. Break them into parts. Use a table like the one below.

Prefix	Stem	Suffix
dis	appear	ed
	march	ing

8.19

Write out the following lines. Underline the prefixes and suffixes.

The town clock started to chime. 'Stand by,' whispered Fliss. Gary reappeared from his room. She could feel him shaking. Lisa switched on her torch and shone it on the door. Swiftly, silently, they padded across the landing. They opened the door and walked into the darkness. At first it was impossible to see. Had there been a misunderstanding?

8.20

Work in pairs. How many words can you make from the following prefixes and stems?

For example: **appear**: *dis*appear, *re*appear; **able**: *dis*able, *un*able.

1 heat **2** fit **3** belief **4** cover

Prefixes: un- dis- re- pre- mis-

8.21

Now make as many words as you can from the following stems and suffixes.

For example: **pack**: pack*ing*, pack*ed*; **soft**: soft*ness*, soft*ly*.

1 kick **2** kind **3** regard **4** fear

Suffixes: -ing -ed -ness -less -ly -ful

8.22

SKILLS
PAGES 60–61

Each sentence below has a word in bold. Add a prefix or suffix to the word. Write another sentence which shows the meaning of the new word.

1 When we went into the room, I was very **afraid**.
I had been **unafraid** up until then.

2 I wanted to **walk** straight into the darkness.
Gary thought that ...

3 We wondered if the vampire would **appear**.
If it did, then ...

Skills

Commas

> **Commas should be used:**
>
> **1 to separate words in a list:**
>
> Dave Roberts bought a tee-shirt, sunglasses, sun-cream and a hat.
>
> *no comma is needed before the final 'and'*
>
> **2 to show where a reader should pause so that a sentence makes sense:**
>
> Then he put his hat on the sun was so hot.

9.1

TRF
PAGE 48

SKILLS
PAGE 41

Write a sentence that lists five items you would take on a snow holiday. Use commas to separate the items in your list.

9.2

Write out each sentence listed below. Add commas so that the sentences make better sense.

> **1** Dave went up the mountain put on his skis skied down the slope and crashed.
>
> **2** Tears ran down his face his leg hurt so much.
>
> **3** After he crashed the snow turned red.
>
> **4** While he groaned and kicked the doctor bandaged his leg.
>
> **5** Before he could get up his skis slid down the mountain.

Apostrophes

The apostrophe shows where letters have been left out. It is used to shorten words that are used a lot and joined when speaking. These are some of the most common:

1 do not → donøt → don't   4 we have → wehǻve → we've

2 did not → didnøt → didn't   5 you are → youǻre → you're

3 can not → cannøt → can't   6 it is → itⱦs → it's

9.3

SKILLS
PAGE 10

Rewrite the sentences below. Shorten the bold words using an apostrophe.

1 We **can not** make football practice tonight. **We have** got to go out.

2 **I will** come tomorrow if **you are** playing then.

3 I **did not** know about the practice. **It is** too late to come.

An apostrophe with an s can be used to show that someone owns something: 's .

Instead of this long sentence: *The shirt belonging to the goalkeeper was ripped.*

you can write: *The goalkeeper's shirt was ripped.*

The 's shows that the goalkeeper owns the shirt.

9.4

Rewrite these phrases so they make sense. Add 's to the owners.

1 The man camera   2 Jim rugby shirt   3 Jo friend
The man's camera

9.5

SKILLS
PAGE 10

Rewrite these sentences. Add three 's to show who things belong to.

At last the referee whistle blew. Ian boots were covered in mud. People hands were sore from clapping so hard.

Paragraphs

Remember to break your writing up into parts or paragraphs. This makes it easier to read. You often start a new paragraph when you change what you are writing about and describe a new time, place, person, action, speech or idea:

	You were writing about	You change to
time	today	next week
place	inside	outside
person	me	someone new
action	deciding to do something	doing it
speech	meeting someone	someone speaking
	someone speaking	someone new speaking
idea	something happens	how it made you feel or what it made you think

9.6 Read the diary entry opposite. Why did the writer start a new paragraph each time? Write down the reason.

1 = new time

9.7 Write a diary entry about a holiday or day out. You could make one up. Make sure you write in paragraphs. Use this plan.

1 When and where you went.

2 What the place was like.

3 How you got on with the people you went with.

4 The different things you did.

5 What you thought and felt about it.

Begin a new paragraph by writing the first word about a centimetre in from the margin.

We finally arrived here on Wednesday at 2pm. The journey seemed to take forever. We'd been trapped on that coach since 11pm last night! A baby screamed nearly all the time. We arrived feeling tired and grumpy, especially my younger brother Tom. I wondered if the rest of the holiday was going to be this bad.

1 By Thursday people had cheered up. The sun was shining and people smiled at one another. There was lots of food for breakfast.

2 Tenerife is a wonderful place. It's alive with brightly coloured flowers. There are lots of bustling tourists in dazzling shirts and shorts. It's hard to feel miserable here for long.

3 My brother Tom raced off to the pool. I decided to go shopping. I needed a new swimming costume. I'd forgotten to pack mine.

4 I set off down the hill. I hadn't gone far when I heard running footsteps. Someone grabbed my arm. I swung round and couldn't believe my eyes.

5 'Sarah, what are you doing here?' 'Mum got a last minute holiday deal and here we are!' My best friend grinned at me.

6 Suddenly I knew this was going to be a great holiday after all.

Drafting and editing

9.8

Follow these steps to produce a really good piece of work. Learn them as you:

> Write a film review for a teenage magazine. Choose any film you know well that is suitable for teenagers aged under fifteen.

STEP 1

Planning

First look carefully at what the question is asking. Make notes to plan your answer. Use the stages below.

ICE CREAM MURDER Certificate 12

A crazy film starring Julia Robertson and Liam Neilson. It will keep you in suspense all the way through. The story opens in the unlikely setting of an ice cream factory in Russia. Richard Earl (Neilson) gets a package in the post containing a computer disk that will (you've guessed it!) cause World War 3 if it gets into the wrong hands.

Julia Robertson (an unlikely undercover American spy) falls for Earl while trying to get the disk back. As you'd expect, a gang of evil weirdos also want to get their hands on the disk. It's got some of the best chase scenes ever seen. All in all, it's a film for action lovers who enjoy a touch of romance too.

STAR RATING
★ ★ ★ ★

1 What have you been asked to write?

Is it a story, poster, diary entry, newspaper article or review? A diary entry is very different from a poster. Think about how it should be written – what are its **features**?

> In this case you have been asked to write a film review for a teenage magazine. Note down its features.
> • heading • columns • summary of plot • star rating ...

2 Who are you writing <u>for</u>?

Is it for adults, a friend, young children, teenagers ...? Writing for a child is very different from writing for an adult. Think about the *way* you will write and the sort of *words* you will use.

> Your review is for teenagers under fifteen. Note down how you should 'sound' ... like an expert? enthusiastic? friendly? serious?

3 Choose what to write

If the question lets you choose what to write about, make the best choice.

> In this case you can choose a film. Note down films you know well and enjoy. Are they suitable for teenagers under fifteen? Choose the best one.

4 Decide what points to cover

Now note down main headings for points you want to cover.

> In this case make notes under the following headings:
> **a)** what is the film about?
> **b)** who stars in it?
> **c)** why is it enjoyable? What are the best moments?
> **d)** who would enjoy it?
> **e)** what star rating would you give it?

5 Decide in what order you will write about the points

STEP 2

SEE ALSO
PAGE 86

First draft

Now write your first draft. Follow your plan. Bear in mind how the piece should *look* and *sound* as you write it. Remember to break your writing into sections or paragraphs.

Write the first draft of your review.

STEP 3

SEE ALSO
PAGE 90

Checking

Check your first draft, and proof-read it. Make sure:

- you have *really* answered the question
- every sentence makes sense, starts with a capital letter and ends with a full stop, question mark or exclamation mark
- you spot and correct **spelling** and **punctuation** mistakes
- you have broken your work into parts or paragraphs.

> First check your draft review using this checklist. Then, in pairs, look at each other's draft and help each other.

STEP 4

Final version

Write the final version of your work. Make it look as good as you can. Proof-read it for the last time.

> Write your final review.

Proof-reading

SEE ALSO

PAGE 89

TRF

PAGE 50

Always remember to check what you have written. Find and correct your mistakes before you hand your work in. Then you will get better grades!

The student below has made some mistakes. Can you put them right? Write out the mistakes with the line number. Show how it should be corrected.

line 1   the film ...   The film ...

Check that:

1   The sentences make sense, start with a capital letter and end with a full stop (there are four mistakes).

2   The other punctuation is correct (there are three mistakes).

3   The spelling is correct (there are six mistakes).

4   The work is broken up into sections or paragraphs (there is one mistake).

the film was called 'Ice Cream Murder'. It starred Julian Roberts and Lisa Neeson. It was about a man caled Richard Earl.

Richard had to find a computer disk. It had been stolen from the government. An evil gang were trying to escape with it.

5   The film started off in Russia in an ice creem factory but Richard travelled all over the world searching for the disk. He never gave up a woman called Tracey Harley was also searching for the disk. She and Richard kept meeting each other in the same plases. In the end they got together.

10   The disk was so important because it had plans for a new nuclear weapon on it. If it got into the rong hands it would mean war. I thought the film was. It had some good chase scenes in it. Im not the only one who enjoyed the film. The reviewer in *Time In* says,

15   'This film has got to be seen.'

He also thought it wass clever the way the film was funny but also scary:

One moment I was laughing and the nex moment I was on the edge of my seat with fear.'

Don't confuse: of and off

Listen carefully to the sounds **of** and **off**. If it sounds like **ov**, it should be spelled **of**. Otherwise spell it **off**.

Use **off**:
1 to mean the opposite of on:
*Tara turned **off** her Walkman.*
2 when someone moves down from a place:
*Then she jumped **off** the bus.*

Use **of**:
1 when something belongs to something:
*Pupils **of** this school must obey the rules.*
2 for a group of objects:
*a row **of** jumpers*
*a school **of** whales*
3 when you say 'Of course!'

9.10

TRF
PAGE 76

SKILLS
PAGE 22

Read the sentences aloud carefully. Decide whether you need *of* or *off*. Write them out correctly.

1 Get of/off the bus at the High Street.

2 Walk past the row of/off shops.

3 Of/Off course you need to cross over the road.

4 Turn of/off the High Street and go into the park.

5 The Lord Mayor of/off London will be there.

Don't confuse: too, two and to

too

If the word means something **extra** then you put on an **extra o**:

*There were **too** many people on the roads.*
*Cycling up hill was **too** hard for me.*
*If we catch the bus instead, I'll come **too**.*

Use **two** for the number 2:

*The **two** bikes were covered in mud.*

Use **to** for everything else:

- as part of a verb phrase (see page 51)
  *John likes **to** ride his bike across the hills.*

- showing where an object is going
  *He rode **to** Brighton and back.*

9.11

TRF
PAGE 76

SKILLS
PAGE 22

Decide whether you need *too*, *two* or *to*. Then write out each sentence correctly.

1 We stopped for lunch on the way too/two/to Brighton.

2 It was too/two/to hot to sit in the sun.

3 Too/Two/To of us jumped in a stream too/two/to cool off.

4 Too/Two/To hours later we reached the sea.

5 I was too/two/to tired too/two/to do anything but sleep.

Don't confuse: there, their and they're

Use **there**:

1 to write about where a place, person or thing is:

The sparklers are over there.

> *Cross off the 't' to remind you it is a place – here!*

2 as part of a verb phrase:

There are lots of people here.

Use **their**:

to show something belongs to them:

It is their firework party.

> *It's got an 'i' in it because someone can say 'I own it'.*

Use **they're**:

when you shorten '**they are**':

They're over by the bonfire.

9.12

TRF
PAGE 77

SKILLS
PAGE 47

Decide whether you need *there*, *their* or *they're*. Then write out each sentence again filling in the spaces.

1 _____ faces shone in the firelight.

2 '_____ going to start the fireworks soon.'

3 'Let's walk over _____ to get a better view.'

4 '_____ brilliant!' Adam said happily.

5 _____ must be hundreds of rockets.

Don't confuse: where, were and we're

> Use **where**:
> to talk about a place
> *That is where Liam Neeson lives.*
>
> *Cross off the 'w' to remind you it's a place – here!*

> Use **were**:
> as the past tense of the verb 'to be':
> *We were standing outside his house!*

> Use **we're**:
> when you want to shorten 'we are':
> *We're so lucky to have seen it.*

9.13

TRF
PAGE 77

SKILLS
PAGE 37

Decide whether you need *where*, *were* or *we're*. Then write out each sentence again, filling in the spaces.

1 _____ is Liam's house?

2 I think _____ being taken there next.

3 '_____ nearly there,' said the coach driver.

4 Soon we _____ standing outside it.

5 'I can't believe _____ doing this,' Anne said.

Don't confuse: who's and whose
would/should/could *have/of*

Use **who's**
when you shorten 'who is':
Who's your favourite footballer?

Use **whose**
for people and things when you want to connect them:
This is Dave, whose favourite team is Arsenal.

when you want to ask who something belongs to:
Whose trainers are those?

9.14

TRF
PAGE 77

SKILLS
PAGE 47

Decide whether you need *who's* or *whose*. Then write out each sentence again, filling in the spaces.

1 _____ playing in the match on Saturday?

2 Mike, _____ favourite position is goalkeeper.

3 My friend _____ staying for the weekend is coming, too.

4 Is that the friend _____ brother's an actor?

When you shorten 'have' it sounds a bit like 'of'.
Make sure you don't write the wrong word down!

They could of ✗   They could have ✓

9.15

SKILLS
PAGE 37

Write out and correct these sentences. Change the word 'of' to 'have' where necessary. Write out in full any abbreviated words.

1 I could of been a professional footballer. I would've liked that.

2 It would've been fun to play for England. I could have been famous.

3 I should of trained harder. I could've played in more games.

4 You would of earned a lot of money. You could've been rich!

Heinemann Educational
Halley Court, Jordan Hill, Oxford OX2 8 EJ
Part of Harcourt Education

Heinemann is the registered trademark of
Harcourt Education Limited

First published 1999
2010 2009 2008 2007
12 11 10 9 8
10 digit ISBN 0 435 10542 6
13 digit ISBN 978 0 435105 42 6
Designed and typeset by Gecko Ltd
Illustrated by Phil Healey, Jeffy James, Desmond Nicholas, Andy Quelch, John Storey, Gary Wing, Rosemary Woods and Gecko Ltd
Cover design by MCC
Printed and bound in Spain by Mateu Cromo

Acknowledgements

Clare Constant would like to dedicate this book with much love to Raymond and Margaret Morgan. The authors and publishers would like to thank the following for their kind assistance in the preparation of material for this book:
David Robinson for supplying information on influences on the English language on pp72–73. The etymological derivations have been selected as teaching examples of how words have entered the English language. No attempt has been made to represent the complexity of word development across languages. Editors of etymological dictionaries may often select a different stage of a word's development through many languages as its root and may give examples that differ from those presented here and those presented in other dictionaries. Further information may be found in *The Story of Language* by Mario Pei, George Allen and Unwin, 1st edition, London 1952. The map represents Europe in the 1990s and not its divisions in antiquity.

Tom, Edward and Henry Bertram for providing material for the transcript on p47.

The authors and publishers would like to thank the following for permission to use copyright material.

World Vision UK for the advertisement 'Every 24 hours for Sakhina is a struggle', p9; Guinness Publishing for ten facts from *The Guinness Book of Records* 1998, p12; Penguin Books Ltd for extracts adapted from the *Book of Banshee* by Anne Fine (Hamish Hamilton, 1991). Copyright © Anne Fine 1991, p15; Yorkshire Television Ltd for an adapted extract from Episode 5, Scene 1, from the script of the Yorkshire Television production of *The Turbulent Term of Tyke Tyler*, by Gene Kemp, adapted by Richard Callanan (Heinemann 'Spotlights'), p17; Rogers, Coleridge & White Ltd on behalf of Jennifer and Graeme Curry for the poem 'The Postman' from *Down Our Street* (Methuen Books, 1987), p19; Walker Books Ltd, London, for an adapted extract from *The Changing Face of Johnny Casanova* by Jamie Rix. Copyright © Jamie Rix 1998, p25; Toby Eady Associates on behalf of Jun Chang for an extract from *Wild Swans* (HarperCollins), p27; Laura Cecil, Literary Agent, on behalf of Norman Silver for the poem 'I Want Trainers', from *The Walkmen Have Landed* (Faber and Faber). Copyright © Norman Silver 1994, p29; Phil Preece for an adapted extract from *Hall of Mirrors* (Ginn & Company), p32; Random House UK Ltd for an adapted extract from *The Dark Stairs: A Herculeah Jones Mystery* by Betsy Byars (Bodley Head), p35 and for an extract from *Twopence to Cross the Mersey* by Helen Forrester (Bodley Head), p80; David Higham Associates Ltd on behalf of Charles Causley for the poem 'What Has Happended to Lulu?' from *Collected Poems* (Macmillan), p37 and on behalf of the Estate of Graham Greene for an adapted extract from 'A Shocking Accident' in *Collected Short Stories* (Penguin), p75; Solo Syndication Ltd for an article 'A cracker of a ring, but 70 years too late' by Ian Cobain from the *Daily Mail*, 24 December 1997, p39; Transworld Publishers Ltd for an adapted extract from *The Story of Tracy Beaker* by Jacqueline Wilson, p45 and for an extract from *Room 13* by Robert Swindells (Doubleday, a division of Transworld Publishers Ltd). Copyright © Robert Swindells 1989, p83; Oxford University Press for an adapted extract from 'Tiger Story, Anansi Story' in *West Indian Folk Tales* by Philip Schofield, p55, and for an adapted extract from 'Magistrate's Tale: Snowy Crow' from *The Canterbury Tales* retold by Geraldine McCaughrean, p79; First Choice Holidays & Flights Ltd for an extract from the Sovereign Worldwide Collection, Summer 1998 brochure, p57; The Society of Authors on behalf of the Bernard Shaw Estate for an extract from *Pygmalion*, p67.

Whilst every effort has been made to locate the owners of the copyright, in some cases this has been unsuccessful. The publishers apologise for any omission of original sources and will be pleased to make the necessary arrangements at the first opportunity.

The publishers would like to thank the following for permission to reproduce photographs on the pages noted.

Tony Stone Images/Karen Moskouitz, p4; Adapted from a World Vision advert, p9; Hulton Getty, pp27, 77; Alban/Donohoe Picture Service, p39; Tony Stone Images/Stephen Cooper, p40; Pictor International Ltd, p41; Transworld Publishers Ltd/Gareth Boden, pp47, 49–50; Transworld Publishers Ltd, p49; First Choice Holidays, p57.

Picture research by Diane May.